BLOWING MY OWN TRUMPET

An Autobiography

MICHAEL FAUNCE-BROWN

Published by Michael Faunce-Brown
Publishing partner: Paragon Publishing, Rothersthorpe
First published 2014
© Michael Faunce-Brown 2014

ISBN 978-1-78222-340-5

Book design, layout and production management by Into Print
www.intoprint.net

Printed and bound in UK and USA by Lightning Source

With thanks to the many people who have nagged me to write the story of my life – I have given in.

One

Who Am I?

THERE WAS A period in my life when happiness went hand in hand with Nature. From the age of four till ten years old I lived with my mother alone on a twenty two acre holding in Devonshire. The nearest habitation was a cottage across the wooded valley with its fine old oaks, and after that a farm house with its bullying occupant about half a mile distant. Ten close brushes with Death were some way off.

My father had volunteered to fight in the first three weeks of World War Two, September 1939 and at first was in Palestine with a cavalry regiment, the North Somersetshire Yeomanry, still mounted on horseback. It was an especially good effort considering he was thirty seven years of age, when most recruits were in their late teens or early twenties. He was also blind in one eye and covered this up at his medical, peering through his fingers. We were only to meet for the occasional long weekend leave over the next seven years. My sisters Wendy and Elizabeth were yet to be born, seven and thirteen years after me.

Our holding lay astride a rocky ridge covered in yellow gorse, good for making camps in which to hide from an imaginary invader, although Mr Hitler had other more ambitious plans including castrating all British males. Ow! On either flank lay the wooded valleys with twin streams, which came together by what was now a little bridge below our house, Metford.

Many happy hours were spent damming a stream to make the pool deep enough to swim in. With no audience save the water rats and an occasional squirrel, one could swim 'au naturel' and dry in the sun stretched on a mossy rock like Mowgli. A rapacious reader, I imagined the wolf Akela and panther, Bagheera guarding me in the shadows cast by shielding trees, friends compensating for the lack of children with whom it would have been magical to share my 'jungle'.

The first thing I can remember of this life was not diving out of the womb with a rugby ball in one hand and the Karma Sutra in the other; rugby, only in that this was the one team sport at which I was remotely successful. I mean Rugby! I remember cutting the hedge aged three with a pair of scissors at my grandmother's house, Smeath Paddocks, near Ashtead, Kent. The hedge stretched for about fifty yards and was over five feet high so I doubt whether I would have finished it fifty years later. Smeath has fifty one rooms with marble pillars in the ballroom. It is now a special school. The butler had his own maid. I hope she was pretty.

This is the boy, who was to travel widely, play in musical groups, run an armoured regiment's motor transport in Jordan, aged nineteen, survive bullets in Amman, teach average ability kids Maths to achieve average A's in external exams, and produce feature and documentary films, in case you want to turn off at this point.

My grandfather on my father's side died before I was born. His engineering firm, quoted on the stock exchange, faded with his death. Father read Agriculture at Jesus College, Cambridge. He knew nothing of engineering so his father's firm was dissolved, leaving the family considerably the poorer. Grandfather Brown invented a cutter for our troops in the first World War to cut through the enemy barbed wire, which held up our advances. I still have the prototype. It screwed onto the barrel of the rifle.

Granny and maiden Aunt Violet moved to a rural village, Collingbourne Ducis, in Wiltshire, a much smaller house with "only" seven bedrooms and an acre of walled garden plus a pony paddock and large lawns. Scissor work may have led to my enjoying gardens but I was lucky not to have removed a finger or two.

I was born on the Old Parsonage Farm, Compton Abdale on the glorious rolling farmland of the Cotswolds of Gloucestershire in 1935. I have a Lionel Edwards picture of the local hunt hanging on my wall. We left when I was only three before I could be thrown out of too many pubs. My parents used to breed horses. Before they met, my mother had a very healthy riding business at Rottingdean along the road from Brighton in Sussex, teaching the children of the well-to-do to ride. 'Do sit up, Algernon. You look like a sack of potatoes.'

There she met and sold a horse to Sir Winteringham Stable, a leading High Court judge, who would be my godfather. He still rode to the hounds, aged eighty one. He was awarded the title: 'The Mercy Judge' by the Press, although he needed protection from the IRA in the twenties, having sentenced indiscriminate killers to lengthy jail terms. He was a very fine man. I never have had any time for bombers, especially those who kill or maim the innocent, including women and children. When young, I visited him in his country seat in North Wales and we shared a long table for lunch. He threw his meat bones to the six adoring spaniels that graced the dining room. Rather like a Saxon Lord.

He told me of a murderer in his household. When out for walks on his estate, a tenant farmer complained of a series of dead sheep. They seemed to coincide with Judge Stable's walks. One day he noticed tell-tale blood around the mouth of one of his dogs. Next walk he watched this dog surreptitiously slink off, disappearing into a field. It returned minutes later licking its chops. On investigation, there was a newly killed ewe in the field. It killed in a trice for the Hell of it. One gets rogue dogs like people.

My mother lost her brother and mother in a car accident in 1931. Her brother, Jacques, was an agriculture advisor in Africa, a very debonair young man. The racing driver and holder of the world land speed record, Sir Malcolm Campbell used the crash as an example in a scathing newspaper article about reckless drivers. This did not endear him to Mother, who now had no relatives left in England, where she was born. Her father's family, the Raoul-Duvals were and still are leading families in France, with a huge number of race horses they have bred for the past hundred years plus. Her mother, Myra-Rosa Adler was married to Roger Raoul-Duval, and Myra's father was William Adler, who made money from diamond prospecting in South Africa. Mother tells of how he had the first two storey house in Johannesburg. I believe he lost most of his fortune not long after in stocks and shares.

My grandfather on my mother's side, Roger Raoul-Duval was the French liaison officer with the Boers in the Boer War and he wrote a well-illustrated book of the war: 'Au Transvaal'. I have a copy with its many photos of the Boer War. I really must translate it some time. It is an historic gem. He met a young war correspondent during the war, Winston Churchill, who was to be captured by the Boers and then escaped.

Roger's brother was killed leading a cavalry charge into German machine gun fire. Roger died of pneumonia in the same war. More died of illnesses than from bullets. He is mentioned in glowing terms several times in General Jack's Diary. A little eccentric, he used to drive his estate's fire engine fast around the village, Genillé, near Tours, ringing its bell furiously, as one does.

The practice was to keep hundreds of ducks without water and then to shoot them as they flew towards their lake on release. Hardly sport! Their family live in a pretty chateau now, with considerably less than their original thousand acres. A first cousin of mother's, Henry Couturié used to play Polo for France. My wife Daphne and I visited them while on a trip back from Spain. They showed us round their beautiful chateau and we noticed they have a set of table silver matching ours. The Queen stayed with them when racing was on at Chantille. I have a photo of her being driven by Elizabeth Couturié, mother's first cousin.

Another close relation, Marguerite, married Bertrand, the Count de Tallyrand and they live in another chateau where they let poor children stay for holidays; such hospitable people. He passed away recently. They have one thousand acres and many race horses in the family tradition, also one hundred acres for hunting and shooting wild boar.

Further back in time a direct ancestor was Le Say, a leading French economist, responsible for Say's Law: "Supply creates its own demand."

Yet another ancestor of note was Ferdinand de Lesseps, the famous creator of the Suez Canal, who also started the Panama Canal, to be completed by the Americans. He had seventeen children by his first and second wife, two surviving till 1937. In the Hollywood film, Suez, he was termed a bachelor! Who cares about accuracy!

My nanny was sacked for forcing me to eat spinach! It was probably not her only transgression. I may have thrown my plate at her. I see those plates rate highly on the Antiques Road Show. Even if I had seen into the future, I still would have thrown the plate. Actually spinach and poached eggs go down rather well these days – down my throat, I mean. One employee also left when discovered stealing silver teaspoons. And no, she was not transported to Australia! A favourite saying of nanny's was: 'Eat up your food. Think of all those starving Russians.' 'Logical?' I used to think: 'Well, give it to the Russians. They'll know where to put it!'

Mother's Alsatian, Echo, refused to let the doctor near me when a tiny baby. I'm not sure who ruled the family! Aged about two, I was left in a smart hotel bedroom on my own and found a loose piece of wallpaper. It peeled off in a satisfying manner and my parents had to pay for redecoration of the whole room. I prefer paint, these days. In retrospect, perhaps they should have left me in a playpen, those useful devices that used to stop errant toddlers drowning themselves in pools. How did the playpens disappear? Perhaps parents found toddlers like me too costly?

I write the occasional poem, when inspired. For the under-fives:

Creatures Under Wood

I like creatures under wood.
Creepy crawlies ain't half good!
My mum says I really should
Leave them well alone.

Logs are losing all their bark;
Woodlice, field mice in the dark.
I like toadstools in the park.
Here's a funny stone.

Over there's a mound of ants.
Oops! One's crawling up me pants.
Here comes Mum. She raves and rants.
Always got a moan.

Only playing in the mud.
Why blame me? It's in the blood.
I dammed the river... caused a flood.
Time we were going home.

During the early part of the war I was left with my dear Aunt Alice for a year while mother drove taxis in the smoking ruins of Exeter, since she had no money. Aunt Alice rented the Digby's large house, Haydn Gate, in Sherborne. I remember beating a toy drum as my cousins, Anne and Susan and I marched round the school room, to the tune of Onward Christian Soldiers, their governess Miss Moysey, playing on the piano. I was aged six. Probably this laid the foundations to my playing various instruments today. "Christian Soldiers' Rock?" It has a certain appeal.

I had a recurrent dream. A well-dressed fox with a shotgun over his shoulder, would stride into our dining room on his rear legs. Then, mercifully he always stopped. Perhaps this was inspired by the fox hunting I witnessed even younger, over the Cotswolds rolling country.

Father having volunteered for the army, whether an inspired bid to fight for King and country or to escape from Mother and me, I never found out; he left her with no relations or support. It did mean peace on the Devon front for six years. His last words to me were: 'Look after your mother.' I was four at the time and hardly remember him till he returned in 1946. Occasionally we received postcards of the pyramids or a slowly chewing camel gazing at its photographer with laconic contempt. I later had one of Mussolini as a sweet little child. Well, I suppose we all were once!

Father disappeared, only to re-surface when his regiment returned from Egypt, some months later, and wasted away a year or more guarding the Yelverton airstrip in Devon against surprise enemy attack. He visited us one dark night riding a bike down the steep hills from Tedburn St Mary. I don't know what caused him to fall off but he ended up in hospital, his good looks considerably altered. Drunk in charge of a bike? No, be charitable. His torch batteries probably gave out.

Dad off to fight Mister Hitler

Two

Betrayal

AGED SEVEN, I had my tonsils and adenoids removed. That was my first experience of adults lying. 'It won't hurt much and will all be over in a day or two,' they told me, as I struggled against the ether they were pouring inside me. When I came to, my throat felt on fire and it remained thus for four or five days. They tried to make me eat jelly and ice cream, but it felt as if the operation was being repeated. I have this peculiar sensation of feeling pain revisited on seeing operations performed on TV. Very odd! I have often wondered if they had their adenoids removed, would Jews not speak through their noses and snorers stop snoring!

Having moved to Devon, my parents bought Metford, déjà vu, a comfortable three bedroom house, with parquet floored lounge and Persian carpet on which I played with my O gauge trains, and in a playroom for me. It had a pink carpet, which I ruined as I spilt some black dye and in a mad panic, tried removing it with water. My parents were very understanding and probably had a private laugh, later. What the dye was doing there, I have no idea, but it stayed. It is probably still there.

The laundry was a huge copper heated by a wood fire underneath. Clothes would be put through a ringer, which squeezed them dry. Mother would sweep the carpets, which were wall to wall upstairs, firstly spreading used tea leaves over them to keep down the dust. I learnt later this was a commonplace practice.

I had a beautiful toy fort, complete with corner cannons and a moat plus draw-bridge. I used to shoot off the heads of my toy soldiers, now worth a fortune, if complete with their heads. They were perfect replicas of Lancers on their horses and are most sought after. Oh the foolishness of childhood!

The little cottage across the valley was owned by the Patons, a pleasant couple from South Africa, who made their living by buying old places and doing them up, a practice I was to follow in later years with satisfying results. They moved on. Apart from them we might have been living on a desert island. No car, no phone. Oil lamps provided lighting with their tall glass chimneys, some quite sought after as pretty antiques nowadays. Mother would clean them with newspaper so vigorously they would shatter, and a candle took me to bed; shades of Christopher Robin. Come to think of it, she must have been vigorous, the amount of crockery we got through.

I returned to Metford, nearly sixty years later, on a nostalgic trip, to find more recent owners had neglected to paint it and the original exterior is now covered with a green mossy tinge. A wooden chicken house like contraption has been added to the once smart facade. Around twenty old cars litter the paddock to the front of the house. The pine trees I used to climb have lost their branches almost to the top and look like sad telegraph poles, and the pretty garden is non-existent. It looks like a squatters' paradise – not mine. Never go back!

Remember there were no neighbours or visitors. Aged five, on a warm summer day, I wore an Indian's feather headpiece and nothing else. As it got cooler, I cut up a hessian seed sack and with mother's help, made arm holes and wore that. It probably was for just a day or two. Being on your own is not such a misfortune. It makes one resourceful and inventive. Psychologists say that such a situation helps develop Creativity. This makes sense. If one does not have a TV to act as baby sitter and brain-washer, you have to use your initiative or stagnate. Give a toddler an expensive toy and what does he do? He plays for hours with the box it came in.

In the days before we learnt basic biology, aged about five, I remember being worried that my thighs were rounded, not straight. Deformed? A year or so older, how is it that I have two testicles one day and then one disappears for a day at a time.

Snakes abound in darkest Devon. Grass snakes can grow to a metre long and are harmless. Once on a trip to Wales with school children, we were motoring back to camp in a Land-Rover with its spare tyre on the bonnet as they used to have. Suddenly out of this tyre reared a large grass snake. The driver nearly drove us off the road in shock.

We were on our way to Arthog, where a huge quarry had been hewn out of the rock. The only way in to the pretty lake inside was through a tunnel of about fifty yards in length. We inspected it and then returned to camp to go "light weight" camping. I have a photo of a slight eleven year old carrying his "swag" almost as big as he was.

Back at Metford, the field up the hill in front of our house was covered with rocks and clumps of gorse, that yellow flowering prickly plant. When our successors cleared the area, where I used to play so happily, they found masses of adders, only eighteen inches long but with a very nasty bite. Father killed an adder with a spade as it blocked the steps leading up from the road, and another on the compost heap. Only seven people are said to have died from their bites in the last hundred years in Britain but when the neighbouring farmer in Sussex years later, was bitten as he lifted a hay bale, his whole arm turned black and swelled to twice its size, a very nasty experience. The same year I killed an adder on our garden compost heap, close to where our toddlers used to play.

It is curious how in Australia one is forbidden to kill a snake, which intends to kill you, and the Hendra bearing fruit bat is also protected. They descend in their hundreds of thousands on a locality and pollute it with their droppings, so residents have to up and leave. They are responsible for a dangerous and fatal disease, killing man and horses, but we must protect them. A weird mob indeed! Sharks also have their supporters.

I vividly remember hearing Exeter bombed. I was sitting on my mum's knee by the fire being read to from Kipling's Jungle Book. Distant thumps of bombs might have been confused with the natives' drums as they tried to smoke out Sher Khan, the tiger. The bombers only needed three nights to turn a half- timbered city into a glowing ruin. It smouldered for three months. Probably the devastation helped make room for car parks. One bomb landed on Exeter cathedral. It bounced off the roof and failed to explode. This convinced many that God was on our side. Later, Plymouth was flattened in months of relentless bombing. Was God on holiday? Next to Devonport, the Royal Navy base was a tempting target for the Hun. If you go there now, you will find the centre composed entirely of ugly concrete buildings, with the skeleton of St Andrew's church left to remind us of what had been. Such was the destruction that people left the town at night and slept in ditches in the countryside for safety. Signs had to be put up to tell the surviving locals what street they were in. What a wasteful war, as always. But it had to be fought if we were not to become Hitler's slaves.

While speaking of Devonport, a leap into the future: my cousin Rosemary and her husband John motored up the estuary in 2001 in their little boat with me as a witness, reviewing the fleet. We came quite close to what remains of the British navy that once ruled the seas, until a police boat warned us off. It was gratifying to know that at that time Britain still had over thirty frigates as well as their four nuclear submarines. Each frigate has huge fire power, so remember that before you get too greedy around the Falklands again, Argentina!

Three

Pony and Poacher

RETURNING TO OUR home, still six, I had a piebald pony called Imshi, a rude word in Arabic. It had a mind of its own and soon I was being dragged, one foot still caught in a stirrup, through nettles and brambles. Oblivious of my swollen legs in my short shorts, Mother was furious when I hit the pony. She expected me to clean its tack, bridle and saddle, and to help muck out its stable. No wonder I feel slightly contemptuous of children today, when they moan about having to leave their i-pods and TV god to tidy their rooms.

The pony was more acceptable when harnessed into its trap, a rickety two wheel device, which carried the two of us at a trot down the narrow Devon lanes. A whip with a silver band resided in a holder but was never used. It looked impressive! These lanes are still about one car width with passing places every quarter mile or so. Cars had to give way to us as backing a pony and trap any distance was a non-starter. However to meet a car was a rare event. Petrol was rationed and few could afford them.

My only companion, lasting two or three visits, was the poacher's son. He taught me how to snare rabbits. We would search for rabbit runs in the grass, his brown face quivering like a weasel. It was best to rub earth on your hands so they would not smell you. 'Don't forget to hammer the peg home,' he warned. I could imagine a rabbit proudly wearing a shiny human 'necklace' and boasting to his bunny friends about his trophy. You set it vertically in the high grass where the rabbit hops. It strangles itself. Not a pretty idea but a quicker death than the brutal steel jawed trap, the gin, that usually broke their legs as they lay screaming through the night, to be found lying stiff next morning, or sometimes still struggling. Foxes would get caught in these evil devices, too. Thankfully they are illegal now.

Seven years old, I was given a little mouth-organ. I knew a few tunes by heart and tried out, 'You Are My Sunshine'. Ponderously I kept at it till familiar with the notes. 'Swanee River' came more easily and after a battle with some more tunes, I found I could play. Not quite the same as now, with the wails contrived by various mouth and cheek positions, but mother was encouraging and hidden behind a gorse bush, no doubt the snakes found them exquisite.

In Devon's isolated haven, war was remote. Fighters occasionally flew overhead, on their way to cut off German bombers as they streaked home having released their messages of death, but Plymouth and its neighbouring naval base, Devonport were accessible from over the sea and once Exeter had been flattened and burnt, there were no other targets of interest, so few planes.

My first school was a tiny one or two class concern. I stayed there briefly as I believe I had fights with village kids, when I was six. Tyson eat your heart out! As a child totally lacking aggression at that point, my difference in speech and behaviour may have attracted hostility with the other children and I was soon deposited with Aunt Alice. The Devonian accent at that time was practically incomprehensible to outsiders. It has improved over the ages into quite an attractive burr.

When our hens stopped laying, I would collect a dozen dark brown eggs from the Pope's farm half a mile down the Crediton road, beyond their steaming dung heap. Before the days of robust cartons, it was quite an achievement to get them all home unbroken. The total hourly traffic might be a tractor or delivery van. Some grocers and butchers did a healthy trade when country folk were without cars, and buses. What were they?

We had a Jersey cow providing cream, milk, and butter. Mother used to leave the rich milk in huge shallow pans, heating on the stove. As they cooled, the cream separated to the surface: The famed Devonshire cream, so thick and delicious on scones with strawberry jam... A contrast to boarding school fare, where the meat was probably horse, grey and unappetising, and a tiny cube of butter was our weekly ration. No oranges for seven years. We mixed salt, mustard and pepper to spread on our dry bread. There was no obese child in the school; a message for nowadays. Potato cakes and fishcakes were also part of our home diet, and very good they were.

There were workmen sawing down the oak trees across the valley one sunny day. Cautiously I watched these intruders working a good few tree lengths distant. One kind fellow, taken by the feathers in my seven year-old's headband, softened to the young 'Indian' and told him to come back tomorrow. My obedience was rewarded by a beautiful hand axe carved out of the hard wood. It must have taken him hours and was my greatest treasure for some years.

Dogs played an important part in our lives. I am convinced that if I had arrived in this world with large teeth, a lolling tongue and a bushy tail, I would have been much more acceptable. One of my tasks aged seven was to feed the six Springer spaniel puppies. One day I entered their walk-in super kennel, with everything bar a Jacuzzi. They were inspired to rip my new school shirt to pieces off my back. To them it was a great game. It happened so quickly, I had no chance of escape. No time to blink. It was a chastened and tearful little boy who went to explain how his brand new shirt was now in ribbons. Mother could hardly blame me but telling her was an ordeal. I still loved those soft brown and white bundles of energy.

My sister, Wendy was born when I was seven. Hardly a playmate but she had a sunny disposition. I longed for a companion of my own age, but school had to suffice. Elizabeth arrived a further six years later.

I learnt to ride my bike, with father's support, on a rare return from the war. Unfortunately a week later I did not practise using the rear brake and hurtling down the slope to the ford, I put on the front brake and cart-wheeled gracefully over the handlebars to skid along on my knees in my shorts. Two American soldiers appeared and kindly asked if they could help this ungrateful, bloody urchin. I stiffened my six year old upper lip and abruptly rejected their kindness, too proud to be helped by "Yanks". Bleeding profusely, I pushed my bike up to our house. Mother washed the grit out of my knees and used iodine to disinfect the wounds. Yes, it hurt, stung like b----y. The deep scars are still there to prove it. What on earth were the soldiers doing in darkest Devon, with no apparent transport? We'll never know.

We had a neighbouring farmer, who appeared at our house one day and tried to bully my mother into letting him our fields. She told him "no" and when he became abusive, I remember my delight when she let our Alsatian round the door. The farmer was last seen sprinting for dear life down the lane with Pasha in keen pursuit. I wish I could draw the cartoon. For all I know, they are running still.

Four

Southey Hall Prep School

A PREP SCHOOL for boys aged 7 to 13, Southey Hall, was evacuated to safety in deepest Devon at Fulford Manor, near Dunsford after a bomb landed on their porter's lodge in Surrey. Mother and I were driven in a taxi along Devon's convoluted lanes trimmed with primroses. It felt like going to prison since there could be no escape and our weekly letters home were carefully scanned for any references to the 'enemy'. The taxi deposited Mother and me outside the huge studded door of the massive crenellated house. Another victim for sacrifice! Mother hauled on a black metal bell pull and the door was opened by the Headmaster. He was about thirty five years of age, tall and good looking in an Errol Flynn way. There was a feeling of sadness and loss as the taxi took Mother home.

I joined the ranks, of sixty boys aged between seven and thirteen for the next six years. We had a headmaster who played an excellent game of tennis and practiced his forehand on the bared buttocks of the small boys for the slightest misdemeanour. One eight year old, an angelic little boy, was always in trouble. I have often wondered what he grew up into? My own fate was comparatively safe, as I was top of my class in History, taught by the Headmaster, and I had a strong sense of self-preservation...Well, not always! There was no point in telling our parents in the holidays of our beatings or the bullying. There was no alternative school and I doubt my mother would have believed me. Some dads, who had got out of the war, would probably say: 'It'll do them good. Make men out of them.' Or 'Not half as bad as in my day.' Shortly after my arrival, in full view of the school, some older boys made me fight a slightly taller boy, Nigel, and I planted a lucky one on his nose, causing it to bleed. That was the end of that and we became good friends. No more was I subjected to the cock fight. Worse was in store.

A new matron replaced the 'Dragon'. Mrs Hicks was kind and efficient. She was accompanied by her two sons, who were equally pleasant. She indulged the sick room incumbents with jellies and countless puzzles and playing cards. The Head still insisted on us older boys having a cold bath every morning, and he checked we were in the water for about half a minute. Heaven knows what his purpose was. Cleanliness also comes with warm water.

Fulford Manor was recorded in the Domesday book, 1086, and still stands today, occupied by the original Fulford family. They have sons, who should keep alive the tradition. The present incumbent had the foresight to use his beautiful ballroom for conferences and has smartened up the huge house, which must have cost a bomb. It is built in a square with a courtyard in the centre, large enough to turn a coach and four horses with ease. It is three storeys high and built of clay, horsehair and probably an element of dung, as they all used to be. The walls are almost a yard thick. Painted a mellow shade of yellow, it now looks much more friendly. It is set in a beautiful park with a lake and old trees gracing its banks. In our time, much of the park was wild with brambles, stinging nettle patches and marsh; more of that later.

The teaching staff consisted of the Latin master, Mr Lee, a kindly old man, an English master, who walked with a limp and a fierce but kind hearted Maths lady, Miss Houlston, who had taught the Head, so she had to be ancient ! When I wrote to her as a young adult, Miss Houlston sent me some Bath buns. Very nice they were too.

The Head taught History, making it enjoyable by reading to us accounts of battles, Agincourt and the like. The image of three thousand Welsh long-bow-men sending forty eight thousand arrows per minute into the packed ranks of the French, bogged down in the mud, in spite of being so afflicted by dysentery, they fought with their trousers down, somehow appealed to our horrible little minds.

There was also Mac, a young man waiting to go to university, who I think taught Geography. He once broke a wooden ruler over my knuckles hitting them sideways, because another boy coughed and he thought it was me, for which I hardly forgave him; also the French master, who had a short fuse, ("a quick temper" – for Aussies!) and became beetroot faced when his frequent tempers raged. Having a half French mother, who frequently conversed in that language with me, I found that subject no problem. We were fairly advanced, reading Les Miserables aged twelve. Perhaps we felt we had something in common with Victor Hugo's creations. In 1999 a university student told me they were reading the same book at University. My one venture into a French play was only all right on the night after Mr Locke's understandable despair when I just managed to say: ' Mon dieu! Qu'est-ce-que c'est que ce passe ici?' On reflection it might have been easier to say when drunk. Try it some time. I have always chosen to be behind the scenes or producing plays ever since.

There was no Science, but Latin six times a week! This meant my even-tual total failure in Science at Marlborough College and a safe O level in

Latin. Think of the other languages we should have had time for! It only took us a year to learn German from scratch. Some will pontificate about the virtues of Latin as a base for other languages. How much more sensible to learn those languages without the albatross of a "Dead" language around our necks.

Still about 8 years old, I caught a six inch perch in the lake with a bent pin and a piece of string. The kindly cook fried it for my dinner. It may be a case of selective memory but no one else caught anything. I also learnt to swim in the lake in record time, as I cared not for the mud between my toes, if I stood up in the shallows.

On Sunday mornings we would walk to church and try not to snore through the twenty minutes boring sermon. We were each issued with a penny for the collection. I still have a few. In summer our caps were replaced by straw boaters. The return trip was fun as we placed our boaters at just the right angle so when we walked fast down the hill, they would take off and chaos ensued as owners tried to claim their own.

The dormitories where we slept had bare wooden floors. They were heated by black, smelly paraffin Tilley stoves, which struggled to raise the temperature a couple of degrees. As a dorm captain, I was responsible for the younger boys' behaviour. Once a term we would have a dorm feast, of sweets saved through the past weeks. To avoid being caught, I raised a floor board outside in the passage, so it squeaked when trodden on, giving us time to dive into bed and pretend to be sleeping angels if the Head or young master looked in. My story telling must have started here as I used to make up instant horror stories, egged on by the others. I can still visualise being trapped in the turret as red blobs drip from the ceiling!

We had our share of bullies. L---t was a twisted boy, who left the school to go to Dartmouth Naval College, where we were delighted to hear he received some of his own treatment. On Saturday afternoons, when there were no lessons and Sundays after church we learnt Survival lessons in the undergrowth of the park. A member of staff would come with us and sit and read the paper, oblivious of the horrors taking place around him. One friend of mine was tied upside down to a tree bough with a rusty chain. We were dragged through the brambles and generally softened up by boys older and stronger than us, led by L... They made me swallow rabbit droppings, forcing my mouth open like the Gestapo. To outwit our persecutors, three of us made a cave under clumps of rushes. We were hiding in one when a bully boy actually came and stood on top of us, never aware of our trembling presence.

Shades of the Viet Kong! With such experiences, is it any wonder that I feel vicious when bullies of any sort are around?

There were lighter moments, such as during Scripture lessons, taken by ancient but kindly Mr Lee, I would line up three miniature brass cannons on my desk, aim them carefully at the teacher, raise my bible and fire all three simultaneously, using my ruler to flip the triggers. Then head down into my bible, reading studiously. Their matchstick cannon balls never exploded. He never reacted much, thanks be.

There was more freedom to do as we liked, sometimes for the better, others for the worse. Bullies now, if anything, are even more evil. We are so sterile, away from the mud and tussles; we pick up every ailment around. We are the poorer for all the politically correct protection. We mustn't play football in the streets and so don't win the World cup anymore! We aren't clipped behind the ear by the local bobby for some misdemeanour, so go on to do worse. Everything is available on Net, so we don't have to puzzle it out ourselves. We have play stations so we can learn Violence and contempt for the weaker. Respect for fellow creatures and older folk has evaporated. Is this progress?

We would make boats out of Plasticine, with air tight compartments, so they would float, and a wisp of cotton wool soaked in paraffin or methylated spirits sticking out behind, would make them go along. We fashioned cotton reel tanks, powered by twisted rubber bands and cut notches in the wheels so they would climb steep slopes. We made paper darts with folded paper, a piece of rubber as a weight and a pin stuck through the rubber. Accurate and potentially painful!

Conker competitions or horse chestnuts were a popular game. I let mine keep till hard and then they would decimate the competition. A popular way of passing boring Latin lessons was the great marble run. In every desk was an ink well. One could drill a hole under it big enough for a marble to drop through. By carefully stacking books inside the desk, one could make a series of channels for the marble to run from one side to the other, to eventually pop out of the dust hole at the bottom. It was important to pad the ends of each run to avoid tell-tale thumps; quite ingenious. We also played board games like "Dover Patrol" where one had to sink enemy ships or their submarines, and L'Attaque, invented in 1910, where one had to capture the enemy flag. Good practice for future Generals!

I caught every bug possible and as they were deemed infectious for three weeks, I missed many months of education. I suffered Mumps three times;

impossible? Not for me! Whooping Cough, Measles, Chicken Pox, and later at Marlborough, Scarlet fever, when I fainted into the arms of that delectable young nurse. What a waste! At least this bored child became adequate at building card houses and the games of Chess and Draughts. After missing so much schooling, I only scraped into Marlborough but jumped a form at the end of the first term.

The boarders were mostly from Surrey and hundreds of miles from their mothers. Dads would be in the armed services or fire brigades damping down the blazing buildings of Hitler's blitz. So we had several boys to stay from time to time. It was wonderful having a playmate and my mother made them very welcome on long weekend breaks. We may not have had much to offer them but better food and an escape from "Colditz" compensated for having little to do.

With no petrol or transport, matches against other schools were non-existent till we returned to Surrey. Team games in Devon hardly happened. Like hurricanes!

Five

A Port In A Storm

MOTHER'S MONEY WAS all in France and worth nothing, so suddenly we went from being comfortably off to poverty. Father's army pay was not worth sending home and so she let the house and we lived in the valley in a caravan. After Exeter was blitzed and smouldered for three months, she drove taxis. A fare, Mr Cornish made me very rich and happy when he gave me half a crown.

Staying at Haydn Gate, in Sherborne, Dorset with my father's sister, Aunt Alice, the kindest of people and a very good mother substitute, was great. I see from old postcards that this lasted a full year. It had a large garden with huge yellow fir trees, where a six year old could hide from the Indians. That was a happy time.

Aunt Alice's husband, Brigadier John Lumley was away fighting with his cavalry regiment or brigade. As the younger son, he just failed to become Lord ... Staying with them after the war, I found him remote. He would read the Times at breakfast, as one does; he seldom talked even later in the day. I was probably a gauche young man, unworthy of his attention. Raised in darkest Devon and then even darker West Wales, I probably lacked the finesse of the aristocracy, even if I knew not to tuck my napkin under my chin as ignorant film producers portray the British. His study had an immense and beautiful tiger skin, complete with head, stretched over most of the floor, a relic of his hunting in India with the 13th/18th Hussars. The three flights of stairs had many pictures of pig sticking and hunting tigers off the backs of elephants. The tigers seemed to win some of the battles, judging by the Indian beaters dangling from their mouths. One has to feed the dear beasts some way.

My cousins, Anne and Susan lived in the dowager house that once belonged to Lord Devon across the way in Powderham castle. Anne was friendly like her mother. Susan lived for her horse and looked down her nose at lesser people. Visiting Aunt Alice in my teens, I was allowed to show visitors around Powderham. On pressing a secret button, a section of wall swung out to reveal a hidden room, probably used to hide the priest in Elizabethan days, before hunting foxes was in fashion. One day, when fabulously wealthy, I shall have a secret room, to which I can retire and sample the odd glass of

Johnny Walker black label, to write best-selling film scripts. In the meantime there is a similar secret room in my film script and novel, "Slave Children".

1947 was the coldest winter of the century. My mother took the rocking horse off its rockers and made a sledge. Then she trudged over ten feet of frozen snow to get provisions from Tedburn a small village, a mile and a half distant. The ten foot banks of earth on either side of the road had vanished. At school the tall black paraffin heaters were useless and we were given a fourth thin army blanket, which we wrapped round our mattresses so they folded round us, keeping us warm enough for sleep. During the day we wore corduroy shorts and blue knees. Thick woollen jerseys helped. During breaks, we would snowball and toboggan down the hill towards the frozen lake on tin trays borrowed from the cook. When too cold to be outside, we huddled round a log fire, toasting chestnuts and our faces.

Father was still away, his seventh year in the army as the government could not demob all the servicemen at once. The unemployment would have been colossal. There may have also been wariness of Russia.

Six

Return to Surrey

IN SEPTEMBER 1947 the school returned to Southey Hall, Great Bookham, Surrey. I was eleven. A cousin of my father escorted me across London from Paddington to Waterloo stations. He was the son of a General and did not speak to me all the way. What does one say to a small boy!

Southey Hall was a fine Georgian building set in some twenty acres fringed with some fine old cedars, and also deciduous trees. In Autumn we were set the marathon task of raking up their leaves into piles to be burnt or composted.

The house dated from pre 1626 when bought by Lord Howard of Effingham's family. It was first a school in 1924, started by Mr H.R. Fussell. While the school was evacuated to Devon during the war in 1942, Canadian troops were billeted there and they burnt the banisters for firewood. They also chiselled some initials into the marble columns in the ball room. The thought of the building being demolished about 1955 reminds one that there are worse vandals among our paid officials than the graffiti lads on our streets. There is an interesting Web site providing some insight into the building's history and photos of the school.

We were allowed to grow two square metres of vegetables each. Radishes were a favourite as they popped up quickly and tasted nice. Cress would grow on damp blotting paper. There could not have been much nutrition but it tasted fine. Really our pleasures were simple but involved more positive action than gawping at a play station half the day. They encouraged creativity, to be realized later. We created a little village out of sand, kept damp by an overhanging tree. Then populated it with Dinky toys, now worth a fortune.

I discovered a way into the walled kitchen by entering the coal chute from outside and popping up beside the heater in the greenhouse. Stolen grapes taste far better than those watery things bought in a super market. I only confided the way in to one other boy, Richard Reynolds. Discovery would have led to dents in our posteriors from the Head's shoe. Richard recently emailed me having led an interesting life to date, somewhat similar to mine. His tenacity, leading to success at Oxford University, might well have stemmed from determination to taste the grapes.

In my last term at Southey Hall, it being a fine summer, we seniors aged 12/13 were allowed to swim in the pool in the nuddy at night. The water seemed warmer and an extra swim was a treat.

My feeble efforts in cricket: I never learnt to watch the ball onto the bat till my last game, against a very proficient team of 13 year-olds, when I scored 27, retired. Once I tried to swipe a fast black shape sweeping by me, a swallow! I also bashed a close fielder on the head, quite unwittingly. He had crept up unseen on my leg side and the first indication I had was seeing him lying on his back with a growing bump on his forehead. Luckily he lived. The master in charge of the game must have been asleep, not to have noticed him so close. Rather like the batsman!

My father turned up to play in the parents versus the boys match. He scored some quick runs, to my surprise and gratification, and then launched a ball into the stratosphere. He was caught by an Indian boy, a natural cricketer called Bracken. 'Bracken'! I thought they were all called 'Patel'. I still see that ball disappearing into the sun. It deserved to be scorched. The catcher should have made his national team.

One day I was being chased by a 'friend' with compasses and their two inch spike. I will never know if he really would have stuck it into me. As I slammed the classroom door in his face, my hand went right through the glass and incredibly there were no cuts or punishment. My parents may have had the bill for a new pane of glass, but I was surprised not to have been beaten or even told off.

While out of bounds one day, in a wooded area, someone shouted 'cave', (Latin for Beware). As I ran to safety, I failed to see a strand of barbed wire in the shade. It pierced my lip right through and I needed stitches from Doctor Everett, father of the boy with the compasses. They hurt. The Head said I had had enough punishment so he must have had a kinder trait.

On long summer evenings, when it was still light to nearly ten o'clock, I would read in bed, listening out for the tread of Mac (the knife), the young master, whose bedroom was just up the passage. Later in the year there was an invasion of pencil torches, smart silvery gadgets, ideal for reading under ones blankets. Perhaps if everyone left school nowadays able to read, they would enjoy the escapism to exciting events on deserted islands and in eastern bazaars and not have to go around sticking knives into each other. I see the comics we used to read and then chuck away can be worth many hundreds of pounds nowadays – even thousands.

At weekends the Head would leave our dormitory doors open and light classical music would waft up the grand staircase from below. Our subconscious took on a love of music as we waltzed in our minds to Strauss or soaked up Beethoven. A subtle brain washing that I shall always be grateful for.

Some of us were taught to box, aged twelve, by an old navy pro. He taught us how to twist the punch so you cut your opponent. In an even fight against Paterson, who became a naval officer, we could not raise our arms in the end. Whacked!

There was a late entrant when we returned to Great Bookham in Surrey, called Hooper. He was some months younger than me and about the same size. He loved to be deliberately provocative like when he refused to get off my tuck box when I wanted to open it. In the ensuing struggle, I got my arm round his neck and squeezed. As his struggles ceased, I let go and was concerned to see he had turned blue. He soon came back to life, having given me a serious fright and we remained hostile till I left the school.

He was the only boy in my dormitory to give trouble and before going to bed, he spent three times longer than normal saying his prayers. As dormitory monitor, I was responsible for lights out and would get into trouble if they weren't on time. When he refused to get to bed, I tried physical force and in marched Mr Fussell. No word of explanation was accepted. Down to the study I was marched. Pyjama bottoms lowered. Six of the best landed with commendable accuracy with a ferociously wielded gym shoe. It was a matter of pride to hold back tears at least partly induced by the gross unfairness, in my eyes. Between a rock and a hard place!

It makes one glad that corporal punishment is outlawed these days. Just imagine the crisscross patterns that would be left by modern trainers. Quite an interesting study might evolve – like finger prints; every Head distinguishable.

No, they were not the happiest days of our lives although we had our moments. Justice has a way of arriving sooner or later. There was a rumour that our cane happy headmaster left the land of the living while still quite young when struck by a door flung open as the train was still moving. But actually he lived till over seventy.

Seven

A Soldier's Return

FATHER, DEMOBBED AFTER seven years away, was jealous of me, my mother told me and I probably resented his presence as a stranger. I felt un-warranted fear when I held a number of metal fence stakes upright for him to drive into the ground with a sledge hammer. I had little faith in his accuracy or his intentions. This reflected our relationship when as a stranger, he disturbed our equable lives.

At some stage after the war Father worked for the famous race horse trainer in Sussex, Captain Ryan Price as a stable lad, which meant exercising the horses early every morning and generally looking after them. Before the war he had raced in point-to-points, which were country race meeting over fences, some quite high. I have an amusing newspaper cutting of him in mid-air preceding the horse over a fence. If you attend such a meeting, always bet on the favourites. The bookies know who is going to win and set the odds accordingly. No claims on the author if the system fails!

Mother hid our two shotguns when Father said he would shoot himself. Not a calming influence on an insecure twelve year old. Seven years of war were enough to disturb anyone. He was in our force which kicked the Germans out of Belgium, and at the start in Egypt, when encircled by the enemy. The Yanks punched a hole in the perimeter and the North Somersetshire Yeomanry, still mounted on horses, escaped a long stint in a prison of war camp, or worse. They had to shoot all their horses rather than leave them to cruel locals. Frightful! Imagine the effect on the riders.

Father gave me a treasure, his three colour torch, used while he was in the military police. He also gave me a silver topped riding whip, which I lost and only found when rotted under a tree to my great sorrow. Perhaps the jealousy was not really there.

I must have been a mixed up little boy as I hated hearing my parents quarrel at night, and I smashed the rigging of a very beautiful sailing vessel they gave me, when sent to my room. I can't remember ever being physically chastised. Mother was strict and a strong personality. Surviving at a time before State hand-outs, through food shortages and trying to keep me at school on a pittance must have left its toll. She once said to me: 'I wish I'd been born a man and could have fought the filthy Boche!' Hitler would never have had a chance if she had. She was a good shot with her 20 bore shotgun. I guess she was used to fending for herself and did not take kindly to becoming just another housewife.

Eight

To Pee or not to Pee?

WE MOVED TO my grandmother's house in Collingbourne Ducis, a country village with church, thatched cottages and post office in Wiltshire some ten miles from Marlborough. She had a lovely old house with bags of space, enough for my aunt Mary and her three children to live there too. My cousin, Richard, later to be a colonel in the cavalry, was almost exactly the same age as me, twelve. We played countless games of chess, taking it in turn to win.

One day, before tea, we both wanted to relieve ourselves and imagine our embarrassment as his mother came round the corner when we were competing in peeing the height of a garden wall. 'Tea's ready, boys.... Oh, yes. Er... time to come in.' Dear Aunt Mary was probably the most embarrassed. She probably thought later: 'Well, that's what small boys do.' Or even, 'Boys win over girls every time!'

The house was built round an empty space, which occupied the centre of all three storeys. It was bounded by black steel rods, preventing anyone falling down it and features in my short story, "Mrs Montague's Collection," where she holds captive an unscrupulous antique dealer, set on owning her precious furniture.

There were wood panelled bedrooms, once for the servants, in the third storey, and very snug for us youngsters. The kitchen was vast with an Aga stove and large copper pans hanging from hooks above it. There was the morning room for entertaining guests with coffee and a huge sitting room full of antique display cabinets with silver trinkets.

My grandmother played the grand piano to a high standard. Past family Generals looked down on one with haughty glares.

Our Alsatian was constantly attacked by our cousins' nappy little terrier, which should have had more sense. One day Pasha had had enough and he seized his persecutor by his neck. Aunt Mary broke them up with a bucket of water. Relations were a bit strained between families for a day or two. Dogs are so like people, the little fellow having to make up for his lack of bulk by showing aggression at every turn, like Napoleon or Hitler.

My eccentric Aunt Violet lived with my grandmother and during the war, all able bodied women were meant to assist in the war effort, working on the land in that area. Violet simply tended her mother's garden and avoided any effort at all, especially as a local man was employed to do the heavy work. She really just existed all her life, with the exception of tasks like doing the flowers in church. She really was a pillar of the church and I half expected it to fall down on her demise. Aged sixty plus, she announced: 'I feel I could get married now,' but she never did. Being wondrous fat, she probably was out of the race.

Nine

To Darkest Wales

WE BOUGHT AN old Standard Car, which often failed to start. We moved to a caravan in Cardiganshire, west Wales. I slept under an awning next to the caravan. It was summer and all seemed serene. A strange woman lived in a railway carriage on top of the cliff in the same field. It was a first class carriage with beautiful shiny woodwork. I often wondered where it ended up. ... At the foot of the cliff? Quite a feat in those days conveying the carriage to its position, miles from the nearest railway. No, there were no giant or even small helicopters!

One hot day I was strolling back to the caravan when our Alsatian, Pasha, tied up nearby, bit me in the face with no warning or reason and I was blamed. I had done nothing but walk by towards the caravan. 'You must have done something.' Truthfully – 'Me, never!' I have never trusted Alsatians since. Gosh how a face bleeds! It cleans out the germs. How is it that dog owners let their pooches lick their faces, as one sees frequently? Don't they ever see the filth a dog will eat or roll in, given half a chance?

Near our caravan lay the beautiful cliff protected beach of Tresaith. It would be deserted apart from us and perhaps one other family. Nowadays it is well populated and littered with bottles, some broken and even dog excreta. Progress! The next village, Aberporth was where they fired rockets out to sea, a testing range.

The beauty of West Wales I only really appreciated on returning as an adult many years later. The tree filled valleys and rolling hills, populated by cattle and sheep were fit for a Turner painting. Imagine the Welsh archers decimating invading English with their longbows, the winners of Agincourt, Crecy and other famous victories. The Welsh shopkeepers spoke Welsh only except when serving you. They were unfriendly apart from our neighbours, Thomas, who were amenable and friends in later years. We would have to wait till the Welsh were served. Smiles were rationed.

When we first visited the farm, situated exactly where Pembrokeshire, Cardiganshire and Carmarthen all meet, which was to be the family home for fifteen years or more, we were greeted by Daniel and Mrs Adams. He had never been more than thirty miles away from home in his seventy years.

A cultured couple with friendly smiles, they welcomed us with a beautiful crusty round loaf out of the oven, built into the range chimney. Mrs Adams cut me a slice, with the bread-knife towards her ample bosom. I trust she never slipped! Daniel had a strange handshake as I had not heard of masons at that time. There were hooks in the kitchen's ceiling from which hung shoulders of bacon. If you have not tasted home cured Welsh bacon, you have not lived. Nearly a centimetre thick, cooked till slightly crisp, it is delicious.

One day when the cattle cake had not been delivered from Cardigan, ten miles away, Daniel had walked there and then back again with a hundred-weight sack on his back. There's character!

We moved into our new property, Nantsaeson. (Englishman's brook.) Things were pretty basic. The loo was located in a tin shed over a stream. You could watch the fish below. Strangely they were never on our menu! An ex submariner was our plumber. He placed a collection tank higher up the stream. I hoped the neighbours did not also discharge into our stream! We would collect drinking water from a spring spurting out of a rock, summer or winter. It never failed and was always pure. With the incessant rain, we were never short of water.

The sound of rain beating on the window panes at night, while tucked up in bed was almost as good as watching the flames flickering in the log fire. Clothes had to be dried in the kitchen on a line, heated by the Rayburn stove. At breakfast we would make toast through its open door, making sure the slices did not fall off the fork into the glowing coals. The larder – no fridge – was fitted with Welsh slate slabs for shelves. As the breeze filtered through the fly screen window, the slates kept the temperature down. There would be large brown earthenware jars full of eggs kept fresh in salt solution. If one floated you knew it was bad.

The bottom field of three acres was filled with rocks and we never found any use for it, apart from keeping about twenty geese for Christmas. Poor things, they paid with their lives for presents, the tree, the meal and not much else. It is hypocritical to feel too sorry for them as they were merciless bullies of us children, till we learnt that if you run after them, with a loud roar, they'll soon be put to flight.

Our farm house had two double bedrooms and a little one between, mine. A fourth was wedged under the eaves. The bathroom and loo were next to the kitchen, on the other side of a thin wooden partition. The kitchen come living room was heated by a Rayburn anthracite burning stove and the sitting room, by a log fire. We only used this if we had visitors or at Christmas. Our friends were few as working seven days a week and never taking a holiday is not conducive to meeting people.

Country life in ideal conditions beats the town every time. The wind ruffling the golden corn fields and the owl hooting at night, or the bark of the fox all have their own magic. Larks on Salisbury plain, climbing higher and higher as they sing their way out of sight.

Come harvest time, neighbours helped each other. I remember going round to help the Bowens. At lunch-time, the men all sat down and ate in silence, served by the women. Not a social lot. My job was to feed the corn sheaves in at the top of the chute. The threshing machine shook alarmingly and I was warned several times about not letting my arm be sucked down the chute, me to follow. As the corn was nearly used up, men with sticks clubbed the escaping rats, while others shot any missed further away from the action. About this time some farm labourer was sucked through a hay baler. Best not to imagine what came out the other side!

When planting a corn crop, barley for the cows, Father would sow vegetable seeds at the end of the field, so we had a valuable crop of cabbage, cauliflower and the like. In a tiny field beyond our garden he planted raspberries, which grew fast and furiously in the frequent rain, and provided many pots of jam and lunches. Aged thirteen, I drove our little Ferguson tractor to plough one of the top fields, edging my way between rocks, which were scattered like confetti. In spite of driving in bottom gear, I still broke a plough shear. Another task was to slash with a sickle the three feet high thistles, which spread as only thistles can, their seeds flying hundreds of yards in the wind.

Father would often miss the milk lorry, up too late, accidentally on purpose as he could then visit the pub on the way home from Whitland, ten miles away after he had chased the lorry on the tractor.

Mother was convinced that Father had given up his drinking. I came across a pile of gin bottles three feet high in a windowless room in the dark at the rear of the cowshed. His rows continued with my mother. He became verbally abusive towards me only, so Wendy, now six and baby Elizabeth were secure.

Ten

A Killer Or Two

I WAS GIVEN a 4.10 single barrel shotgun and enough ammo provided I averaged one kill per cartridge. I would wait till two or three rabbits were in a line and then squeeze the trigger; three for the price of one. Thomas the trapper caught 180 rabbits, the next night, 120, and then only 80. He did not consider it worth coming again. He probably sold the rabbits to Thomas the Butcher and may have celebrated a good catch with Morgan on the Organ in the local pub.

If not controlled, rabbits would eat all the grass. None would be left for the cows. Likewise the Pigeons ate the seed corn unless we shot them. They were good for pies, like the rabbits. Throw in some onions and carrots plus a turnip. Stalking rabbits taught me patience. I have waited an age for them to come out of their burrows and then shot one. Pigeons were super cunning. They knew to a yard the range of my gun and would eat the corn until I was forty yards distant. Then a cloud of blue grey swirled into the next field. Controlling the rabbit population was absolutely vital as five rabbits eat the same as one sheep and two will breed one hundred and twenty a year, counting those bred by their young and so on. There would be no grass left for our cattle.

Father was a good shot. He had a twin damask barrels 12 bore shotgun and although he only had one eye it worked well, as he could kill at 80 yards. He had lost the other getting a thorn in it while ferreting rabbits.

Before the war there was a terrible train crash, and Father was in the newspaper for 'heroic work saving others.' His volunteering for the army only twenty one years after the terrible first World War showed patriotism and courage.

The gun had protruding hammers, which would go off if caught by a branch or bramble. So I made sure to always walk behind him. He taught me gun lore, such as always emptying its chambers of cartridges if climbing over a fence. And never firing if one could not see what was behind the target. In those days gun fatalities were common. Many people died when scrambling over a fence without unloading first.

We had rabbits in every bank, earth and stone constructions dividing all the fields. So shooting was not our only controller. We would net every hole we could find and then put a ferret down the hole. If the ferret did his job, rabbits would be bolting out of all the holes, only to be caught in nets. Of course, if we missed a hole, the rabbits would all escape through it and apart from the odd one shot on the run, the rest would run away, probably laughing their eyes out. Sometimes the ferret would kill a rabbit down the hole and refuse to come out until it had feasted its fill. Then we would light a fire over one of the holes and a smoke bleary ferret would emerge, licking its lips.

When at Metford, a ferret bit Father's finger and would not let go. I can still see him swinging it round his head in futile parabolas attempting to rid himself of the vicious little beast. People sometimes keep ferrets as pets. They stink and they can turn very nasty, so I do not recommend it.

We only had 10 milking cows, some young stock, 120 pigs and 200 hens, in deep litter. Not much of an income, with cattle cake twenty pounds a ton. By way of comparison, a farm labourer would only be paid about four pounds a week, and our fifty acres plus house cost around four thousand pounds. Father could have earned more working for the council but he valued his independence and enjoyed the land. The hens were at first out in the fields in movable units holding twenty five each. Then a fox got in through a hole the size of ones fist and slaughtered the lot, just for fun. Hear that, the anti-hunting league!

Raynard the Fox

I'm Raynard the fox,
Poor pretty me.
I killed five lambs today.
Don't hunt me.

Raynard the killer
I kill for joy and fun.
Killed thirty hens one day
But only gobbled one.

Sally the grey mare
Would jump the blooming lot.
Next week's the last she'll know;
She's going to be shot.

Black Jack, king of the pack
He has no use no more.
'fore you pull the trigger
Wait till I'm through the door.

The towny politicians
They think they know the lot.
When all is concrete jungle
They all ought to be shot.

My worst task was pulling up frozen fodder beet with frosty fingers, aged fourteen. (What alliteration!) Then there was the electric fence to move every day, so the cows had a new ration of grass. Later it became the practice to have a back fence, too, so the grass behind the cows had a chance to grow again.

Rats were a pest, eating from the grain sacks in the barn. We put down a sheet of iron, left over from constructing corn bins. Then we killed hordes of rats by firing at the sheet as the pellets spread to fan out one night.

Our Siamese cat was a character. It would hunt at night and leave its prey, often just the head, as a tally on our door step for us to discover in the morning. They were always laid out parallel with mathematical precision. I once put the cat in a corn bin where many mice were feasting. Faster than you could blink, it had a mouse in its mouth and one under each front paw.

Our spaniel gun dog Flash and Pasha, the Alsatian would take off into our neighbour's woods chasing foxes or rabbits, or merely having a good time as they barked the good news. Flash gave birth to six fine puppies, which sold very well on account of their pedigree, one going to Ireland. The haunting sound of the steam train to Cardigan would drift up the valley through the woods.

There was a remote cottage hidden in the depths of the woods. It had no road nearby and was the perfect hideaway for an old crone, who asked Mother for a job. She employed her for a few weeks, cleaning the house and doing the laundry till some of our silver ware disappeared. Then, so did the 'witch'.

Initiation
(From my book: *"Tom In Trouble"*)

Witchcraft dark, wing of lark,
Wrap me in thy cocoon,
Bathe me in light of moon.
Protect and guide my mind.

We are now of one kind.
In the shadows of the night
Follow Mercabe's ghostly light.
If I seek the world of day,
I'll soon become Webster's prey.
I give myself to witchcraft's art
For the coven, here's my heart.

"Tom In Trouble", written for all ages eleven to ninety, is about a twelve year old boy, whose engineer dad gives him a prototype tunnelling borer with a vital part missing. Tom finds a replacement part from a scrap heap and gets the machine working. He comes up in the middle of a bank raid, which he foils, and is stolen with his 'Whirler' by crooks intent on using it to steal a rocket from an army arms dump. Plastered up by the crooks to join statues by a stately home, he ends up locking the crooks in the coal cellar.

After other adventures, Tom is caught by witches itching to have him as a trainee warlock. To discover his fate, buy the book from Smashwords.com as an e-book for only $2 or read it in Toowoomba library. At twelve dollars fifty, it won't break you and many adults have found it entertaining.

My parents attended the local agricultural shows. I helped shampoo the cows and pattern their hair. If you won those coveted rosettes in a show, you could sell your breeding stock well. Wendy, and later Elizabeth won several times with their ponies.

Travelling actors put on plays at Crymych, a little village some three miles away, perched at the foot of the mountain that attracted frequent rain. Mother invited the lead, John Gordon home for tea several times. He had a certain charm and came from Spondon in Derby. The actors must have had prodigious memories as they played a different play every night. I enjoyed his company as he treated me like an adult, and he had a sense of humour.

We had no phone or electricity. A petrol engine drove the milking machines. A rough track ran for half a mile from the tarmac road to our house. The last hundred yards were down a steep hill, and every time it rained, the slope became rougher as a torrent flowed down the track.

While searching for hens' eggs in the hay loft, a wild kitten bit my finger to the bone. I only wanted to stroke it! One day I found our Alsatian with a wild cat clinging to its chest and another on its back trying to scratch its eyes out. It was on a losing streak till I chased them off.

There was constant rain even in summer. Fields became a muddy morass. Father was clever at choosing three consecutive days of fine weather to make the hay. Even then, some years, we had to hire a machine to blow hot air through the barn to stop the damp hay heating and catching fire or just rotting. We turned to making silage, compressed fresh grass, which could be added to daily, if it were not raining. It had to be compressed by driving the tractor over it, a hazardous job as it could tip. I can still smell the sweet scent. Black treacle was added to tempt the cows and as a supplement. My finger would accidentally stray into the sweetness.

On a positive note, during summer months there were blackberries growing in our hedges all over. Wonderful for pies and jam. You just had to avoid their thorns, which were just as evident. Hazel nuts were tasty if you beat the squirrels to them. In autumn, mushrooms were plentiful. Rhubarb flourished in the garden, a bonus of the wet climate. There were some elderly apple trees that provided enough for apple crumble. Less welcome were the horse flies, the size of a large bluebottle. The first you knew of them was a sting and a large lump swelling fast on your exposed flesh; legs, arms or the back of your neck.

11

When A Cow's A Bitch

We had a cow called Veronica. It was a bad tempered Ayrshire and more than once kicked Father when he was trying to put on the milking cups. Once it kicked him back against the cow-shed wall. When it calved, it tossed the newly born up into the air and killed it. Veronica had to go.

I enjoyed feeding the calves we were rearing from a bucket. At first you had to put your finger in their mouths to make them think it was their mothers' teats. They quickly learnt to suck from the bucket; so sweet at that age like most young things apart from birds.

We were constantly short of money and yet my sisters had ponies. I never understood the logic. I would not want one. My mother was a great worker but she admitted she had no business sense, and she controlled the purse strings. It was this control that gradually weaned my father off his forty cigarettes a day. I used to still hear his smoker's cough replicated in my son Chris' efforts to smoke himself into an early grave. Thank God he has given up.

We shopped weekly in Cardigan ten miles away. Crymych, the nearest village, had little to offer except for farm machinery. I would be given a shilling to go to the cinema and watch Roy Rogers about to fall off a cliff. He must have had the most amazing luck as next week, behold, he was back there again, ready to trade blows with the bad men and Indians. They never ran out of Indians. We always had a decent meal in a café, in spite of being 'broke'. I also was given pocket money, one shilling and six pence I seem to recall, per week. I would save up to buy treasured dinky toys, now worth around £120 each. To think I gave away around fifty when my parents moved to Bedfordshire and I had nowhere to keep them.

I wondered why the old Welsh women looked at me as I strode down the Cardigan High Street. At thirteen years of age, with all my hair, I was not so bad looking then, believe it or not. Whatever happened! Maybe their interest was my obvious Englishness, as they remembered the invasion by Edward 1 in 1277. I remember it well. He had 15,000 men including 9,000 Welsh. Not really my fault!

When my parents went to an agricultural show or to town and left me behind alone, I would worry as to what would happen if they had an accident? All the cows to milk, the pigs to feed and the hens, plus collecting and washing the eggs. Heaving huge buckets up the hill to the pigs, I did not mind, although I wondered if it would stunt my growth. Mucking out the cow shed was dirty, smelly and not my favourite task but cleaning out the filthy old sow's pen with that evil smell that stays with one after several washes; that was the pits.

12

Marlborough College

LOCAL EDUCATION WAS in Welsh, so I was sent to Marlborough College in Wiltshire, even then one of the great Public Schools of the country. It had around 800 boys. When I arrived aged 13, my parents had put my name down too late and I had to sleep out at Mrs Lowe's, down town. This was the school that produced Sir Francis Chichester, who flew from Britain to Australia, only the second to do so, in a Tiger Moth in 1929 and sailed round the world single handed, in 1967, aged 65, with a stop, at Sydney, the first to do so, in the Gipsy Moth, now on show by Greenwich museum. If he had been more than one and a half degrees out with his navigation in the plane, he would have missed a vital little island north of New Zealand and must have perished.

Soon after our arrival our housemaster, Mr Coggin, had all the new boys round for tea. Then he put on a record of the American Maths professor, Tom Lehrer, with his wonderful songs about the hunters in the Bush. "If it moves, you shoot" and at the end of the day your trophies were: 'One game warden .... and a pure bred Jersey cow.' Come to think of it, they haven't changed much now.

Marlborough, as well as countless bishops, produced Sir John Betjeman, one of Britain's finest poets and Sir John Hunt, leader of the first successful Everest expedition. Also Sir Anthony Blunt, the master spy, who worked for the Russians for twenty five years and who was responsible for the Queen's Art gallery. It seemed it did not matter whether one was good at Art or Exploration or even Spying for the Russians, one was knighted or benighted!

Rather easier on the eye is Old Marlburian Kate Middleton, Prince William's Princess. He shows good taste. Kate has that unassuming but confident trait probably enhanced by her time at Marlborough.

Marlborough was the first school in the UK to have girl and boy boarders 13+, possibly the first to have a metal workshop capable of building a fast go-cart around 1950, and a leader in Business Studies. It was known for encouraging a liberal attitude and thinking for oneself, rather than the sausage machine reputation of many Public Schools of that time. Boys were allowed to cycle for many miles provided they informed their housemasters of their routes and some would cycle the twenty six miles to Stone Henge on midsummer's eve, to see the sun come up over the altar stone. No sacrifices were recorded!

In its early years, the eighteen forties, Marlborough College boys often had fights with the town lads, no doubt jealous of them. There were bars on all windows facing the town. The junior 'A' house and senior 'B' houses were built in squares with a hollow centre and had bars keeping boys from falling down them. Before my time there was an initiation ceremony for new boys, where they stretched a blanket across the void and bounced the thirteen year olds across it. An end was put to this when one missed the blanket and died in his fall. In my time we only had to get up on a table and sing. I can't sing so that kept it short. I think it was "The Boy Stood On The Burning Deck."

So why did I not make more of myself? Partly cursed by many months off school, as mentioned previously, did not help or boost my self-confidence. Living in the countryside away from all human contact apart from mother, must have reduced my immune system to zero. If there was anything worth catching, I caught it. It certainly did for my German O level, as we only had a year to learn the lot. No Science at Prep School was a disaster.

A selective memory, which favoured Maths and foreign languages, meant that different types of rocks formed a concrete block in my head in Geography and remembering Shakespeare's plays was second fiddle to Biggles and Hornblower. I used to complete my two Prep's each night in half the time and surreptitiously read a novel, not remotely connected with my lessons for the rest. I was beaten for this by our dear housemaster, George Tarleton, once a great hockey player but then weakened by Parkinson's disease, so one feared his cane not a lot.

I was also beaten for walking and not running in the cross country run. Two prefects had to watch while a third gave me four strokes, which were clearly not meant to hurt. I said: 'Shall we get on with it, Gentlemen,' when they seemed loath to start. I was fourteen at the time, and already a low key rebel.

We had Highland dancing as one activity. I remember doing the sword dance with bare feet. The swords, laid in a cross on the floor of the gym, were probably not very sharp but it kept you on your toes and attached!

We had one boy boxing for the school called Bacon. He would take off in a fight like a windmill, punching so fast his opponent had no chance of reply and was usually lying horizontal in the first round. He was a red headed fury, and an experience to behold.

The Memorial Hall, able to hold the whole school at one sitting, was built on a marsh, on a concrete platform, which goes up in winter and down in summer; quite an achievement.

Swimming was in an old canal, cut off to make a general swimming area plus a competition stretch twenty yards long. It was concreted but as the season progressed, the water took on an evil dark green hue. It was only cleaned out once a term, as the temperature of the fresh water was below 55 F. At 56 degrees, one could dive in and skim across to the other side, to spring out and lie gasping in the summer sun. We all swam in the nude and the local girls were said to congregate on a hill with binoculars. There could not have been much to observe in that temperature. The only time we wore costumes was in inter school matches.

I remember coming a poor fourth, up against much bigger boys in the backstroke. It was the only time I ever met our Headmaster, known as 'The Magger' or Master. He helped my frozen and exhausted body out of the water, saying: 'You look cold, boy!' The master understatement of the year. On that same hill was found a pile of wine bottles, all that remained from some likely lads, who stole from their housemaster's wine cellar. Perhaps they became wine tasters in later life.

Near the swimming pool is the mound, a fifty foot base for what once was a castle. It was covered in thick vegetation and I never ventured through the jungle to see what was on top. Now cleared, we can see there is nothing much. Sometimes it was called 'Merlin's Mound'. I guess he got around quite a lot of the west country, casting spells here and there. Doing quite well on TV lately.

We all had to join the C.C.F. or Combined Cadet Force. This led to us taking Cert. A. parts one and two. A section of this was map reading and another, taking part in Field Schemes or military manoeuvres in Savernack forest. We learnt how to camouflage ourselves and to move very slowly so as not to be seen. There was the Leopard crawl, oozing flat along the ground and the Monkey run, where one ran on all fours with clenched fists so as not to injure ones shooting finger. It had the benefit later of making one open to officer training while doing the two years National Service and three years in the Territorials in the armed forces.

I secreted a thunder-flash back to school after one such exercise. Waiting till all 120 boys in my year were doing their prep and it was dark outside, I sidled out, unnoticed by the supervising master, and took apart the explosive device used to simulate bombs. I spread its contents along a windowsill and laid a small trail of powder to light as a fuse. I then lit it but the fuse was too quick and it burnt the end of my finger as it exploded in a roar and huge flash. I ran back to the door, furthest from the master as he rushed out the other and when he returned, I was sitting, innocent but in serious pain. I was never caught but the pain of my blackened and cracked finger was a constant reminder of my silliness for several days. And how could I go to the nurse in the sanatorium and seek much needed medical assistance?

When other keen types would be playing cricket on Saturday afternoons, I was away, working on a farm, feeding a pellet making machine, for pig and cow fodder or dismantling a huge poultry complex. This pellet machine comes up in my screenplay and novel, 'Slave Children' when the baddie tries feeding his sidekick into a similar machine. Then I had the same amount of spending power as my richer companions. Every week, I would mow my landlady's lawn, which also helped the coffers. This started in my first year, aged thirteen. If one could sell the quantity of grass I have cut over the years, I would be a green millionaire. An environmental treasure!

One sleepy warm day Mother was driving me down to the station, on my way back to school, about one and a half miles from home at Glyndwr, a tiny hamlet lucky to boast a Halt; not really worthy of the title "station". We pulled up just in time to see the train had come in. I suddenly felt sick. Where was my trunk? We had forgotten it and it must have been back inside the front door. The station master kindly said that the train would wait for us and we high-tailed it back home to fetch the trunk. When we arrived back at the station, the train driver was patiently waiting for us. Where else in the world would this have happened? Such kindness. It was the only train that morning and I should have arrived back at school a day late. I clambered aboard with my trunk and we steamed down the single track. The engine driver had to have a baton to prove his was the only train on the track. Sadly the railway was axed like so many others some years later.

In my last year at Marlborough College, aged sixteen, I actually played cricket in my house team, which visited some local village clubs. It was good fun, even though I never made the Ashes. We were treated to half a pint of beer or cider. Friend Henry, also an early leaver, probably wanted to work on his dad's farm, and ended up very rich as a result of never paying the right price for anything. He even arranged for the council road workers to dump unwanted hard core on his farm when he wanted to build a road across it. Resourceful!

The same term, Henry and I cycled to a local village and against the rules, entered the flea-pit or cinema. Imagine our consternation when we saw one of our younger teachers sitting there. He elected not to see us and we enjoyed the film.

I thank Marlborough for encouraging individual thinking, not being afraid to go against the tide, lateral thinking where the unconventional may be tested, and respect for everybody, at least at first!

13

Castles

WALES IS A little country about one hundred and seventy miles square, with some splendid castles. Cilgerran castle some eight miles east of Cardigan is situated on a cliff edge, with the winding river Teifi at its base. It features in one of my children's books and TV series script: 'Young Escapers'. There is still a fair amount left of its towering stone keep and it is worth a visit for its view of the river through the trees over a hundred feet below.

Raglan Castle, between Abergavenny and Monmouth, is thought to have been built as early as 1070 by the Normans to control the Welsh. It has a beautiful curtain wall and a water filled moat and it is my favourite of all the Welsh castles. Hever, in Sussex, still habitable and used by Henry VIII for Anne of Cleves, is possibly the most appealing in Britain. I enjoyed the golden carp in the moat and the revealing statues lining the walkways to the lake. The torture chamber has its own fascination. The Astor family had the lake dug out around 1905 by several hundred workmen with wheel barrows, just as they brought quite tall trees by horse and cart from as far away as Norfolk. The castle was not large enough for all their friends to stay, so they built a very pleasant mock Tudor village.

Stokesay Castle, in Shropshire near Craven Arms, is perhaps the finest fortified manor house in England. Built in 1291, it is still in very good order. The main hall has never been altered. There is a hole in the roof for smoke to escape from an open fire in the middle of the hall. The half-timbered Elizabethan gatehouse is most attractive. The castle was never demolished as its occupants gave in, possibly to save it.

My exploration of castles led to a boy in my book, "Young Escapers" finding an escaped cheetah in the dungeon of a ruined castle in Wales. He tames the cheetah and uses it to capture his pursuers. There is plenty of action throughout.

14

Bad Times

BACK ON OUR farm, I could not take any more GCE O levels at the local school because everything was taught in Welsh, so my wish to complete Physics, thus opening my future career to a higher level, was 'kaput'. German would also have been easy in a further year.

While waiting to be called up to the army, things got pretty tense at home and having saved up a few pounds, I got on the train to somewhere in desperation and arrived at Swansea, already strapped for cash. I used up my precious Coronation five shilling piece on a meal and failed to get a job at the café. Destitute, I walked the deserted streets that night wondering if there was an army recruiting office in town.

A passing policeman saw me skulking in the shadows and took me to the police station. They were very kind, giving me an empty cell for the night but leaving the door open in case I felt trapped. Also a blanket as it was cool. Next morning they gave me a super cooked breakfast and told me to wait till they contacted my parents. Since we were not on the phone, it took a while for the local policeman to arrive at my home. Mother agreed to pay for my trip home, so I took the next train back. Nothing was said when I got home and it was as if it had not happened. I guess they knew why I had left.

We were gathering in the corn harvest, stacking up the sheaves to shed any rain, when suddenly there appeared our English neighbour and his wife. Earlier my father had politely asked him to keep his chickens off our land till after the harvest. They attacked my parents and as Mr Ball was six inches taller than my father and twice as heavy, there was no contest. But Mother rugby tackled the wife and felled her. I was still only sixteen and had several inches left to grow. My planting a fist in Mr Ball's ample stomach had little effect. They took off home, having made their point. I have always wanted to meet him since, as an adult, but it is possibly best that we never did.

Our other English neighbour killed a sow of ours when it strayed onto their land, as pigs will, by beating it to death with a pitchfork. It may be that both families had taken refuge from the law in darkest Wales. There was little point taking legal action as only the lawyers seem to make financial gain. Funny so many of them take up politics!

I did get to see the Festival of Britain in London with Henry Hitch. We stayed a weekend in town with his aunt and the only event that sticks in my mind was when we visited Soho and walked into a brothel, aged sixteen. We had a quick look around and saw precious little. As a scantily dressed lady approached us, we ran out, laughing.

15

National Service January 21st 1954

– January 21ˢᵗ 1956

ON RECEIPT OF that longed for summons to join the army, aged eighteen years, three months, complete with a free one way ticket, I boarded the train at Glyndwr for the long journey up to Carlisle, close to Hadrian's wall, bordering Scotland. It was built by the Romans probably to stop the Scots from stealing our cattle and us raping their women. More with relief than sadness I sat back in the empty compartment while the little engine chuffed its way along the wooded valley to the main line at Whitland. I relaxed and enjoyed the pictures of our glorious countryside above the opposite seats, courtesy of Great Western Railway.

Hadrian's camp was the training centre for our armoured brigades including those who wanted to join such illustrious regiments as the eleventh Hussars, the Cherry Pickers with their wine coloured number one uniform in armoured car regiments, the eight modern tank regiments or the old heavy tank regiments rich in battle honours, one of which I was destined to join, the Queens Bays, 2ⁿᵈ Dragoon Guards, now amalgamated to be 1ˢᵗ the Queens's Dragoon Guards, with a long presence in Irak, and Afghanistan more recently.

The white barrier to the camp rose with military precision, clanging shut behind us as if to announce our last gasp of freedom and sanity. We were driven past a gleaming guard-house into acres of drill square with some Daimler armoured cars parked near the guard-house. I wondered at their little two pounder guns and speculated that their smoke grenades were probably their best defence. They have a reversible seat and reverse gears that function as fast as the forwards. Thus when used for reconnaissance, if the first shell does not get you, in theory, you slam into reverse and scoot away at sixty miles an hour.

'Out you get, you long 'aired 'orrible lot,' roared a red faced sergeant, oblivious of the fact that he had yet to see what sort of ' 'orrible lot' was about to spew out of the back of the truck. Kitting out seemed to take hours as we received the baggy khaki trousers that we would have to iron into submissive knife edged creases, the itchy thick battle dress tunics and the heavy boots with their mottled leather that would have to be smoothed with a hot spoon into shining mirrors. Did all the original cows have such pimply skins?

We were not much better, our civilian clothes shed and the doctor's very personal inspection over. I had wondered whether he was examining our breeding prospects, but was told he was searching for hernias. Our barracks were single decked corrugated iron Nissen huts with rows of about fifteen iron framed beds down each side and showers, basins and loos at one end. By each bed stood a chair. On the bed part of our kit would be meticulously laid out each morning for inspection.

Some of my companions were straight from the slums of Glasgow. They weren't all the right side of the law. When I managed to lock my keys in my locker and had a minute and a half in which to change from P.E. kit into full battle dress, one of them said: 'Got a pin?' I lent him my cap badge. He bent down and had the locker open faster than I could have with a key. One youngster was from the Scottish Highlands. I don't know whether anyone could understand a word he said. I couldna!

Hadrian's Camp was the coldest place on earth or felt like it, and shaving in cold water every morning must have been a rude shock to those unfortunates, who had never been away to boarding school. Every morning we staggered in to breakfast to face lumpy porridge, frequently burnt for good measure and half cooked eggs that looked at one pleading to be released from their slime, and cold greasy bacon, which should have been delicious. Luckily there was ample half burnt toast, also cold of course and lashings of marmalade and margarine, so hard that it would never spread. No need for a fridge. NAAFI tea must have started life early in the morning. It tasted like dirty sock soup – not that I've had any lately – but at least it was warm.

The first six weeks were spent square bashing. The main object of endless drill sessions appeared to be to stamp Hell out of the poor defenceless tarmac and to lay the foundations of varicose veins. One learnt to appear to stamp, avoiding smashing the heel to splinters. Sergeants were only happy when screaming at you a tirade of endearments at one hundred miles an hour: 'I'm standing on your hair, lad. Get it cut!' irrespective of it having been cut only three days earlier by the army barber, whose instructions must have been to dehumanise us by creating a mob of hedgehog clones.

'That rifle's your best friend. Polish it, clean it, love it.' In the next breath we were told how to smack our 'best friend' in varying modes of brutality.

'One two three, two, two three, three!' All shouting in unison these wonders of rhythmic Maths.

Anyone failing the morning kit inspection would have to double round the square, about half a mile several times with a heavy pack on his back, and if the instructor was feeling last night's hangover, with a rifle held above your shoulder. They weighed seven pounds. Few did this more than once. I not at all.

One evening, for no apparent reason, a thick necked Scot, Macateer, or something similar, invited me to be his sparring partner. He had two pairs of boxing gloves in his locker. Faced by something that looked like an escapee from the gorilla house, I had no option but to learn to dodge very fast. I believe he boxed for Scotland after he left the army.

Later, one of the old Etonians and I were 'volunteered' by a corporal to box in a tiny ring. I whispered that I had no wish to fight him and would pull my punches, but he ignored or misheard me, and suddenly I was fighting for dear life. Having learnt to cover defensively, I did just that, waiting for his energy to lapse or the bell to go, but he had remarkable stamina. Eventually I started to attack and we were both pretty shattered by the time the watchers became bored, there being no bell. Anyhow, we were not invited to box for the regiment. Now, if he had been the enemy, with a weapon, I would have had no hesitation in shooting him!

The most entertaining aspect of basic training was when I managed to convince our Corporal Leece, troop leader, that I would never get my boots to shine, having only had "wellies" down on the farm. He very kindly polished my right hand boot to mirror reflection and then, when convinced that all Welsh boys were incredibly thick – I was always good with accents – the other one to match. I fondly remember our kindly corporal sitting in the NAAFI one evening, drunk as a skunk – as one does – playing Frisbees with a pile of plates, which soared through the air gracefully to explode off the far wall. I hate to think how many months he went without pay to replace them, but there was no reasoning with him.

F-----ing Officer Cadets – Some of us were singled out by dint of having some GCE 'O' levels and having passed our school CCF Cert. A tests, as potential officers. Thus, after six weeks drill and some weapon training for the next six weeks, we were hived off for a number of tests. WOSB: War Office Selection Board. Before this, during Sten gun practice, we were warned that this nasty close combat weapon, produced for two shillings and six pence, was prone to jamming. A recent recruit had his jam. He turned round to show his instructor and shot him dead in a hail of bullets when it decided it felt like firing again. "Look Sarge. It's jammed. --- Okay. It's going well now. Brrrrr. Dead! What a shame!"

During grenade practice, we were told of a brave sergeant who threw himself on top of a grenade. Some paralytic recruit had frozen with it in his hand, having pulled out the firing pin and released the lever.

The knowledge that we were a breed apart made certain of the future troopers, or 'other ranks' hate us. The realization that they might meet us again when we were in charge of them, as officers did not penetrate their enlightened minds. One morning some of us were forced by our barrack room-mates into freezing showers. Seeing that we were outnumbered ten to one, I quickly stripped and marched into the shower, relics of Prep School days, steeling myself against the pinpricks of ice and laughingly invited our persecutors to join us, even clutching a tormentor and dragging him in with me. This had the happy effect of bringing it to a close since the whole joy was to see these "soft f...ing P.O.'s" suffer. Not to be dragged under to get their own kit soaked.

Several of my barrack-room mates were straight from Eton's sixth form and a thoroughly pleasant bunch they were. In some ways, they were more confident, having stayed at school till eighteen with its mentally maturing benefits. Several looked soft but how many of their predecessors had died bravely in the recent Korean war, only months older?

One Stoic, a Stowe public school ex pupil, Martin Instone was a particular friend, having a good nose for the best pubs in Carlisle. We had to be careful of our funds. For the first three weeks we were paid the princely sum of fifteen shillings per week, out of which had to come the cost of boot and button polish. It was best to be cautious in the streets of Carlisle since we were only allowed out in uniform, rather like convicts. Martin and I would avoid certain areas, the haunts of soldier bashing Teddy Boys. These mindless yobs would lie in wait for soldiers and beat them up just for a thrill, and oblivious of the fact that their victims might have been past mates.

All good things come to an end and one famous night after I had left for my officer training, the army took their revenge. They went as a squad into town, found the Teddy boys and gave them what they deserved, a good hiding, using the effective buckled belts and army boots as weapons. It was said that for months you could not see a Teddy Boy in Carlisle.

A failed Medical student was also with us. I don't know what became of him but he taught us a book-full of rugby songs, you would not sing in church, although the vicar might have written some of them.

We were taught to drive on a deserted airfield for three twenty minute sessions each. This was to come in handy when I joined my regiment and was asked if I could drive. 'Right, you can drive us back to the camp,' ordered the Captain. Little did he know I was potentially more dangerous that the enemy. I got into the jeep's driver's seat, switched on the engine and took off fairly fast. All was fine till we came to that right angle bend. One side left the ground and three white faced passengers got out fast, as I came to a halt.

'Have you driven a jeep before, Faunce-Brown?' 'No Sir.' 'Well you slow down to fifteen miles an hour on that sort of bend – not thirty. It's all right. I'll drive the rest of the way.'

At the selection board, W.O.S.B., we were interviewed by two colonels and a brigadier. I came to a smart halt in front of them, thinking: 'I've got no chance.'

'You have five minutes to prepare a talk on anything you like. Over there.'

'Christ, what the Hell do I talk about?' Did I know anything about anything, isolated from the real world in darkest Wales? Inspiration! Pigs and make them laugh. And that's exactly what happened: 'A pig is an animal with an appetite at one end and a smell at the other...' Then I diverted it onto Rough Shooting, and we were away.

We had to take turns leading others across a make believe mine field. I had just seen the excellent film, The Red Berets. They had blasted their way across a minefield with a bazooka, the rocket launcher that could take out tanks. The others were discussing how they would use the barrels and rope we had been equipped with. 'All or nothing,' I thought and offered my solution. Nothing was said apart from surprised looks, but I passed my WOSB.

16

Mons

THE NEXT STEP was Mons Officer cadet school. I remember a yellow Volkswagen travelling too fast up to a corner. It flipped over and almost immediately four officer cadets scrambled out. They rushed round to one side, heaved and the little car was the right way up again. They jumped in and drove off as if it were an everyday occurrence.

We were drilled by the famous Sergeant Major Britain. He could see a cadet wiggle his nose to get rid of an exploratory fly out of the massed ranks a hundred yards distant. His roar was audible a mile away. Two officer cadets were dancing around in the guardhouse both inside one of Britain's belts at the same time when he arrived on the scene. It must have been fun observing the ensuing nuclear explosion. He went into the diamond trade after leaving the army; another hard rock but he had a sense of humour.

We were taught Military Law by an ex prosecutor of the Nazi Nuremburg trials. I only remember one case where a music instructor was had up for assisting a girl pupil's breathing. Say no more!

We had a miniature indoor range with .22's and had to give fire orders such as: 'H.E. cross-roads, ant. 800 yards, fire.' This meant that the loader loaded a high explosive shell to be fired at the range of 800 yards at an anti-tank gun. We also practised out on the range at Lulworth in Dorset. First, we used the 600 round a minute Browning machine gun. I was first to go and scattered masses of rabbits back into their burrows. Then I had to fire at an old tank. One bracketed, which meant firing and if one missed and it went over, you fired again closer. Then you halved the difference and hit the target. I went over with the first shell and then knocked the turret off with my second shell. It hurtled way up into the air, glowing red hot. It was quite an experience.

We then were told a shell had not gone off as it should have done. You waited thirty seconds and then drove forward about thirty yards away from the others. Then, praying that it would not go off in your arms, you ejected the shell, carefully lifted it out of the turret, scrambled out yourself, lifted it down to the track covers and jumped onto the ground. Then you lifted it up, gently like your teddy bear, walked ten yards away from the tank and deposited it carefully on the ground. Then, trying not to hurry, you walked back to the tank, got back inside and told the driver to reverse back to the others. I expect it was a dummy shell but it looked the same as the others. And they were all twenty-pounders, so heavy enough. Come to think of it, only a chosen few went through the process. Expendable?

Oh, yes, the first shell. It went clean over the cliff face and narrowly missed a little freighter sailing into the bay, in spite of the danger flags. I have never seen a small ship do a skid turn before!

I had to do a repeat at Mons, of an extra month. Not expert enough on the indoor range. Well I always did prefer the real thing. Having passed out of Mons, I was now an officer and a gentleman! Funny! My dad was the latter. What had gone wrong with me? I was given a weekend pass to go home to West Wales. There was fog and the journey took nineteen hours. During my five hours at home, I received little by way of congratulations, perhaps because my father had served in the ranks throughout the war.

I joined the Queens Bays at Tidworth, a bleak but comfortable barracks on Salisbury plain. The Bays were the second senior regiment of the British army, with the Royal Horse Artillery the most senior. The Bays or 2nd Dragoon Guards were raised in the time of King James 2nd. Their loyalty to the Crown being unquestionable, they had the privilege of remaining seated when a loyal toast was drunk. Their history is worth a visit on the Web.

The week before, after a party, a young 2nd Lieutenant like me set off a thunder-flash in his bedroom wardrobe. The furniture in his room was reduced to matchwood like his next month's pay packet. Perhaps it was as well that I had had my previous experience and thus was not tempted to emulate him.

17

Service in Jordan

WE SHIPPED OUT to Suez on our way to Jordan and enjoyed some target practice off the end of the ship. Passing through the Suez Canal we were warned about the local youngsters who went fishing through open port-holes and hooked anything they could drag off the ship. They tried to sell us "Feelthy photos of my sister, or me" and were only tolerated till they had delivered some fresh fruit and vegetables.

First thing every morning we all did some P.E on the deck. It was a short trip as Egypt is only about two thousand miles from England. Food was quite good. Eventually we rounded the Sinai Peninsula and sailed north to Aqaba. On landing we found our camp was protected from stealing Arabs by rolls of barbed wire and of course sentries at the gate. There were no permanent buildings but we all had individual tents and a batman, usually shared between junior officers. We had to pay him a pound a week for cleaning our kit, taking our laundry to the dhobi and tidying our tents. Since our pay was only two pounds ten shillings a week, there was little left for Mess bills. These were for our drinks and I soon learnt to keep to orange squash and not to accept other people's 'shouts' if I could avoid them. I had been warned about the expense of joining a cavalry regiment but survived. Come to think of it since they had to pay no mess bills, batmen were better off than I was!

Most of my brother officers seemed to be well off with private incomes. The Welds were big landowners in Dorset. There is the Weld Arms at Lulworth in Dorset. Lulworth Cove is a delightful little sheltered bay, where I have set one of the scenes of "Slave Children", an action film for adults. The innocuous yacht rocks gently at anchor, while awaiting its human cargo.

Some weeks later I tried reducing my drink level and passed out. It was the dysentery that did for me and I ended up in hospital for three days, feeling pretty grim. One had to keep up the body fluids or look out.

Aqaba town was a small collection of mud huts, and stank of dead goats and camels. Flies were abundant. We arrived in summer and in the first week three troopers were hospitalized with sun stroke. The sand was too hot to walk on in bare feet. Most of us lay on our beds throughout the afternoons. Work started at six in the morning and we finished soon after eleven thirty as the tanks were too hot to touch.

Showers were jerry cans, pierced with nails perched above us and warmed by the sun. The toilets were 'long drops' or deep holes dug in the sand. They had a crude shelter round them and were hot as Hades. A plank of wood with a hole in it sufficed as a seat When they had been used a while, the methane gas started to rise. One day a new recruit sat on the throne, minding his own business and smoking happily. He threw his fag end down the hole and there was an explosion. Not nice!

C squadron, to which I was admitted, went almost immediately to our desert outpost eighty miles distant near Ma'an, a few huts with a defunct railway station, courtesy of Lawrence of Arabia, whose men had blown up most of the railway around those parts in World War One. Our camp had a concrete building for the officers and a little swimming pool. What exactly we were doing there, I am not sure but back in Aqaba we were keeping the peace between the Arabs and the Jews. This same railway was further demolished when we used it as target practice. One moment, an embankment; next moment, none. We finished what Lawrence of Arabia started.

We took it in turns to inspect the guard at dusk. Our sergeant major took a delight in beating me to it, so I would arrive to find he had already carried out the duty. So I had dressed up for nothing. It was a harmless game and I kept quiet about it with my colleagues.

There was already a full complement of officers and I was lucky to have been accepted by the regiment. I have often wondered if Colonel Cordy-Simpson at Mons had been approached by my unapproachable uncle, Brigadier Lumley along the lines of: 'Hello, old chap, do you think you can find a suitable regiment for my nephew, Faunce-Brown? How's the polo going, by the way? ...He's a bit young but time'll put that right. The Bays? Yes, they'll knock him into shape. See you at the Cavalry Club? Well done.'

Chatting to some of my troop near Ma'an

18

Ma'an Outpost

So I was added to Lt Jeremy Railton's troop as a sort of spare part. He was a pleasant fellow and more mature than some, who acted as if they were just out of sixth form, or even younger. Two of them had joined the regiment in Germany and seemed 'good time kids'. Our squadron leader Major John Griffin was pleasant and had a sense of humour. He would eventually become ADC to the Queen, which was a great honour.

Much of our time seemed to be spent on tank maintenance and I tried to learn a little of the technical side, particularly how to change a track rod, which might be a little hairy in the middle of a battle. I was shown how but never got round to doing it myself. If a track rod breaks, the whole track can peel off the tank, leaving it un-navigable and a sitting duck. The Centurion tank was capable of twenty miles an hour. It weighed about sixty tons. It carried one hundred and twenty shells, varying from Armour Piercing to fight tanks, High Explosive to take out anti-tank guns and Smoke to cover ones whereabouts, especially useful if the engine cut out under fire.

I made a fool of myself when trying to siphon petrol out of a tank, I can't remember why. Probably to be used for cleaning the engine. I used an opaque tube so never saw the petrol rising till I had it in my mouth and down my throat. I could have had fun as a fire eater but felt pretty crook for days.

The twenty pounder was the latest thing in tank warfare as it was self-righting, in other words, if the tank was pitching all over the place on unsteady ground, the gun would remain level with its target; a great asset. We went out on a live shoot and I am not sure whether I hit the target as we were moving quite fast and firing at the same time, in a cloud of dust.

Eventually Jeremy went off on a helicopter flying course and I took over the troop of sixteen men and four tanks. We went out into the desert for three weeks as solo troops. The Jordan desert is mostly gravel with plenty of dust. I had as sergeant a guy called Ransome, who had been a naval officer. He seemed to always have a good reason for missing out on these desert schemes and so I had only a lance corporal as back-up. We had no ammunition and a man with a pistol could have overcome us at night although we took it in turn to do a two hour guard duty. We slept like sardines or peas in a pod next to each other under an awning stretched out from the tanks.

Nights were as cold as the days were hot, although it was not mid- summer now. I rolled over one morning and out from between us crawled a scorpion, its nasty sting curled up over its back. We were lucky no one was hurt. The desert is almost entirely flat with no sand – just gravel. There was the occasional 'sugar loaf'; a large rock which had failed to be eroded over thousands of years of wind driven sand. So navigation was by dead reckoning. Every so often I would leave the tank to avoid magnetic attraction for the compass and stride off to take a reading. One also kept a careful record of how far we had gone. It seemed almost magical that the colonel found us out in the middle of nowhere.

On another occasion a small snake chased my driver across the desert. He would stop every so often to hurl stones at it, accompanied by our raucous laughter. Eventually it gave up the chase. Towards the end of the scheme we were very slowly navigating over and between giant rocks in a cloud of dust. I ordered all tanks to stop till the dust had settled. However the tank behind me was slow to react and it bent my petrol trailer, leading to a court of enquiry in front of the Colonel later. No one was found to blame. Visibility at zero was a fresh experience.

Cooking was simple. We filled an empty bean can with sand, soaked it with petrol and threw a match at it. This provided a very efficient stove, across which we placed a couple of tank track rods. Virtually all food was tinned apart from dry packets of biscuits and porridge. Water was in very short supply and I am sure we could have been smelt before we were seen! For shaving and cleaning teeth, an enamel mug full was all we had.

The last day of the scheme, the colonel suddenly appeared out of the desert and spent the night on my tank as we continued an advance in the dark. The rest of the squadron, another twelve tanks joined us. No lights were to be shown. We were lucky as another tank near us drove over the side of a wadi, a dried up river bed, and its driver lost his front teeth. Hearing about this, I ordered my troop to advance very slowly and we had no accidents. At one stage I walked in front.

We had duties apart from learning to cope with the tanks and desert. I was Fire Officer for some months and will never forget when we had only left the camp a short while in a Land-Rover when someone noticed a pillar of smoke back in the camp. We high-tailed it back to camp and found a blackened figure being attended to by the doctor, and the battery charging plant in flames. The charger lorry was burning furiously so I seized an extinguisher and put out its tires. Then I pointed it down the petrol tank, praying it would not explode. Meanwhile the REME Sergeant Major Ward was directing the tanks away a safe distance. Eventually we got things under control. Some of our fire extinguishers had not worked properly so the next task was to refill them all. The silly man had tried filling the charging plant with petrol while it was running. There were many large tank batteries and sparks must have been flying so the inevitable had happened.

Luckily for the burnt offering, we had an excellent Doctor, John Pryce, doing his National Service with us. He saved the man although the trooper had over fifty per cent burns. He was air lifted out from the camp by an R.A.F plane and his life was saved. But I hate to think of the agony he must have endured.

We had a traditional party where the other ranks are hosts to the officers, in return for the officers serving them at Christmas. Their aim was to get us paralytic and with me they succeeded. I remember the gin bottle being passed round more often than was good for us. Suddenly a trooper went berserk with an axe and I remember its blade flashing past my head as I took refuge in the toilet. While he was trying to disengage, ready for a fresh pursuit, I jumped into the swimming pool and waited for everyone to sober up. I wonder what happened to the axe man. Surely not the fellow who terrorised Leighton Buzzard years later, not long after the great train robbery?

For entertainment we had films sent up for Sunday showing from Aqaba, together with crates of beer. I was in charge of this for a while. Was I really so hyper active that I got all these jobs? Anyhow I had to collect the money and organise it all and it stopped me from going bananas from boredom.

19

Regimental MTO

SUDDENLY JOHN GRIFFIN told me I was being sent to HQ Squadron. What had I done? I was to become Regimental Transport Officer, just nineteen, in charge of thirty five men and vehicles and responsible for provisions, ammunition and the survival of the Ma'an squadron. I was shown round by the lieutenant who had been doing the job up to now, and had just finished his short service commission. That took a morning. So there I was, with no experience but for helpful Corporal Mackenzie. Well, we survived until there was a general inspection and we failed to clean the vehicles properly before we painted them, so I got down in the dust and showed the men how to leave grease on the nipples before painting, and how to clean off every vestige of dust. A black mark!

Well, it all was concluded successfully in the end. I was not greatly impressed by my squadron leader, who gave me no advice or help throughout my time with the MT troop. At that age, with my sheltered past, I badly needed a mentor, all the fashion these days.

The road from Aqaba to Ma'an was corrugated terribly with no tar seal or concrete and many bends. On one side was a cliff going upwards and on the other a steep slope maybe a hundred yards down a valley. The evidence of drivers meeting a dead donkey just round a bend or simply falling asleep at the wheel littered the route – battered car and lorry remains. One of my drivers had an accident while driving to Ma'an and his three-tonner rolled all the way to the bottom. The cab was flattened to eighteen inches high yet he and his mate crawled out without a scratch. None of us could believe our eyes.

Still in Aqaba, I was given the task of meeting General Sir Charles Keightley, whose son I knew at Marlborough. We had not drilled much for months and I had to learn how to salute him with a borrowed dress sword. After he had inspected the guard of honour, I froze, wondering what the ... to do next. He kindly said: 'You may dismiss the guard now.'

In the afternoons it was so hot that most officers and other ranks lay on their beds sweating. Only the other doctor, John Ross and I went down to the point, close to the Saudi Arabian border and enjoyed some of the best underwater fishing in the world. A turtle looked like a mini submarine and a manta ray stretched for ever, a Vulcan bomber. The colours of the fish were spectacular, bright blue, yellow et al. and I often wondered at the others' lack of interest. Nowadays, across on the Israeli side, at Eilat, they have attracted large numbers of underwater explorers from worldwide. Such were the heat and the rough conditions that all wives and girlfriends had to remain in England. They must have been overjoyed when the regiment, after eighteen months in Jordan, left for Cyprus.

Some of us were invited to a mensif or Arab feast and we sat on cushions on the ground and were given generous portions of goat meat and rice, with herbs. John Griffin, as leader of our party, was awarded a great honour, a sheep's eye. He conjured up a hearty swallow and palmed it into his pocket, which he showed us later, to our amusement.

Around the camp on the mountain's side was a fifteen foot storm ditch. It only rained for three days while we were in Jordan, but in twenty minutes a wave of water gushed down and filled the ditch, swamping the camp. I waded round to the colonel's tent to find him perched on his cabin trunk, looking miserable and surrounded by water. Thousands of pounds worth of food were destroyed and the band lost their drum skins and uniforms. The Colonel's Champ, a super four wheel drive vehicle, was set in the mud next morning like a robin in the icing of a Christmas cake. That was Colonel Bill.

Colonel Charles Armitage took over eventually. He had had three tanks shot from under him in World War 2. That has to be a record in survival. I had a soft spot for Colonel Charles as he offered to lend me one of his polo ponies and to teach me the noble sport. Inhibited by my lack of money, I declined with thanks. Another very pleasant man was Captain Ian Hodgson. He lent me a squash racket and we played many a game in the sweltering heat.

20

Middle East Exploration

A KINDRED SPIRIT arrived, John Morris, also a National Serviceman and at the end of our tour in Jordan, we holidayed together round the Middle East. I think we only had about fifteen pounds each. It started by us flying up to Amman in one of King Hussein's doves, little seven seaters. We stayed the night with two English women who provided Bed and Breakfast near the airport. Then we stayed at the Continental hotel, where we were holed up for two days. There was rioting in the streets and we heard the mob thudding on the hotel's door, trying to break it down. Luckily it held. We stayed in our room, sitting with our backs to the walls between the windows to avoid the odd bullet. Eventually we managed to persuade a taxi driver to rush us to the Lebanese embassy as we needed visas to visit Beirut and Baalbek.

We were driven round a corner into a wide street to come face to face with a howling mob that had just stoned a British colonel to death, we heard later. Our driver did a handbrake turn and we left them to their fun. After waiting two hours for the Lebanese embassy clerk to deign to help us with our visas, we set off for Beirut and Baalbek via Jericho and Jerusalem by taxi. We had a soldier with loaded rifle as a guard. Passing close to Jericho we saw a car being stoned by a mob, its windscreen shattered. Luckily they left us alone. This was a time of unrest as Egypt had just shot down two Israeli planes and in Jordan, in March 1956, King Hussein dismissed the British trainer of his forces, Glubb Pasha. Incidentally the Web has a fascinating description of Glubb's long influence in Jordan and how he started and trained the Jordanian Frontier Force, bringing its numbers up to sixteen thousand men during World War 2, but that is another story. British influence in Jordan was waning.

Just to illustrate how knife edge the political situation was, some American oil prospectors arrived in Aqaba and we were not allowed to protect them when a small mob drove them away. I was privately fuming when their tents and possession were being burnt and I was told: 'No way can we interfere.' It would have only taken one tank to swing its gun towards the mob to scatter them.

Back to Jerusalem, John and I found the Casa Nova hostel run by nuns. We had nice cool rooms with tiled walls. All who have experienced forty degrees Centigrade all day will relate to the pleasure of such a room. We were served a simple meal of home-made bread, cheese, salad and home-brewed wine from their own grapes.

The old quarter of Jerusalem was administered by the Arabs and the new by the Jews. It seemed to work in those days. We followed the path of the Cross, the 'via Dolorosa,' which Christ had carried before being helped by a soldier. It was up and down sloping cobbled streets with bazaar shops selling leather goods, vegetables, and tourist souvenirs such as copies of the cross, or chips off the original, enough to stock a forest. Heavy aromas arose from herbs, soaps, donkeys... We entered the Damascus gate and eventually found the Dome of the Rock with its millions of blue and gold mosaics.

We entered the Church of the Holy Sepulchre, where Christ was thought to have been crucified, and saw the cave where Jesus is meant to have been buried. We bought candles to support the church and no doubt the priests, who were doing a roaring trade with wonder faced tourists ready to believe anything. A strident female American voice shouted from above: 'Wilbur, Wilbur, we've done this place. It's Bethlehem in twenty minutes.' God bless her. She makes me laugh every time I remember her. We next drifted through beautiful olive groves to the Garden of Gethsemane, where Christ was betrayed to the soldiers by Judas for a few pieces of silver. Perhaps I exaggerate here. The groves were pretty scanty.

While exploring the huge walls of the ancient city we met James Money, whose father was Governor of Jerusalem after Lawrence of Arabia. James was a teacher at Harrow public school, where my father and grandfather went. He then joined the Home Office. He was accompanied by the brilliant cartoonist Osbert Lancaster, author of Giles. He was a rotund little man with a natural sense of humour.

Having 'done' Jerusalem and visited Nablus, an olive grove town, its honey coloured buildings interspersed with camels and goats, we arrived in Beirut. This of course was before its civil war and the city, with French influence, was very beautiful. Our real target was Baalbek, at 1,170 m above sea level close by. Its greatest temple was created in the first century A.D. Approached past magnificent cedars, its impressive Corinthian columns and atmosphere of past glories were peaceful. Its one hundred ton blocks of golden tinted stone were lifted somehow up to sixty two feet above ground level. It is now a world heritage site. It was built chiefly by the Romans and added onto by various emperors. Trajan consulted the oracle there. What about, I don't know. Did they have lotteries in those days?

From Baalbek we shared a taxi like sardines, with blaring Arab music and then hitched a ride in a petrol tanker to Damascus. The last left us reeking and tired. The souk or market places stretched across the town. Each stall was back from the narrow street in an archway. As the only foreigners in a street filled with Arabs, some of whom looked downright hostile, we felt a little apprehensive, these two British teenagers out of their own orbit. I bought a couple of bedspreads ridiculously cheap, one for my mother. This may have put us on side with the locals. However we continued to watch each other's back. We stayed at the Palmyra hotel, which was comfortable enough and cheap. Eventually we taxied for five and a half hours back to Amman and flew back to Aqaba. We heard that an R.A.F pilot had taken off in an Arab Legion Dove and crashed it, not knowing how to lower the undercarriage. Not the best way to befriend the Arab Legion.

21

Back In Aqaba

NEXT DAY JOHN and I took a couple of my troop's B.S.A. bikes up Wadi Rum. We shared a large water melon and then threw away what we could not eat. Out of nowhere came a couple of Bedu, who scooped up the water melon gladly. We wondered how many more were hidden in the 'empty' desert? The sand there is very loose and deep and I slid under my bike, with its red hot exhaust. It was very hard pulling myself out with nothing solid to purchase against. This was the only time the bikes were used, to my knowledge. In war-time, they are used by despatch riders with urgent messages, when radio breaks down.

As the heat became more bearable, others would take to the sea on a launch we had managed to obtain. We sailed down the Gulf of Aqaba with an old Arab as our guide, a real character. We would throw a little piece of plastic explosive into the water, which killed many fish we could then use for bait. It was very wasteful as most sank to the bottom. The Arab saw sharks swimming to get their share of the bait. 'You no clefty my fish,' he yelled and leapt into the water, a long knife between his teeth. At which the sharks swam away! No, but luckily they either knew him from previous meetings, or thought the little fish were tastier. Hundreds of miles further south, near Aden sharks would kill at least six people every year but in our area no one was lost. The Barracuda were more feared, with mouths as big as Alsatians and swimming in packs. I only once saw a shoal and created an Olympic record swimming to shore, glad of my flippers.

One day a small pilot fish swam close to Trevor Morris's chest, staying only six inches away and in parallel formation, as they do with sharks. They adopt a shark and live off the titbits it misses. Trevor was understandably alarmed.

The Colonel told us to take turns at the observation points watching the Israelis from 6 to 8 a.m. We never saw anything of interest but it got us up nice and early. They had asked us over for a coffee one morning but we could not go because the Arabs would have fired on us returning.

One of our tank squadrons was to take its tanks on transporters up to Baghdad and hand them over to the Irakis. I suppose they had seen the best days of their lives and it was easier than taking them over to Cyprus, our next posting.

One night I was wakened as I was duty officer, and had to search for Arab thieves, who had come in to steal our old tyres for turning into shoes, and anything else they could lift. They braved our vicious guard dogs and all for nothing. If they had asked the quartermaster, he would have probably given them the tyres. One day a dog handler was seen well bandaged up. He had tried feeding another sick handler's dog. They were not friendly!

In spite of my opting out of polo, Colonel Charles lent me a pony to ride, which was very good of him. We would only ride close to the camp, but it made a change from monotony. We played several cricket matches against the RASC and REME and with John Griffin's help, won the lot.

One of our sergeants lost his stripes as he was putting unopened tins of food in the bottom of dustbins and selling them to the Arabs. It only came to surface when I checked the accounts.

We had one very unpleasant major, who left us early. In Korea he had threatened to shoot another officer for refusing to obey him. Not a great way of making friends and influencing people. I believe another regiment was soon to enjoy the pleasure of his company. Another unpleasant incident occurred just after we arrived in Aqaba. I received a message along the grape vine that a senior officer objected to the fact that when out of uniform, I wore slightly green trousers, rather than the traditional dark grey. I was irked by such stupidity and told the messenger that I would think about it if the objector had the guts to come and tell me himself. That was the last I heard of it.

I heard that the Life Guards were having a rough time in Aden with several men being killed. I hoped my school chum, Anthony Everett was okay and meeting him later back in England, was relieved to find him in one piece.

22

Petra and Azrak

WITH PETRA, THE "Rose red city of Time" only hours' drive north, I took some of my troop up there. We paid an Arab boy to keep an eye on our Land-Rovers and walked off down the Siq, a narrow cut through the fifty to one hundred foot high cliffs on either side. As one comes out into the huge arena hosting once a city of tens of thousands, one is greeted by the Treasury, carved into the rock at the entrance and used in one of the Indiana Jones movies. The rocks are all rose red and the surrounding cliffs are peppered with elegant cave dwellings. A handful of men could keep out an army as the Siq is the only entrance and about two metres wide. It is thought to have been established about one hundred years B.C and was captured by the Romans in 106 A.D. Perhaps they learnt how to abseil down the surrounding mountains.

One weekend eight of us took a couple of Land-Rovers up to the salt marshes near Azrak. We intended to shoot duck and I had my mother's precious Greening twenty bore shot-gun. After a long dusty and tiring journey we arrived near dusk at the mud huts we were to doss down in. Another fellow and I set out immediately to try to bag a duck before dark. We got separated and I soon found myself waist high in rushes and warm water. I shot a duck and tried to find it without a gundog in rushes sometimes as tall as me. I found the duck and darkness seemed to fall at the same time. I had lost my sense of direction. Where was the causeway home to the huts? It was a nasty moment. I would have had a job staying upright in the water and its warmth would make one feel drowsy. Drowning was a real possibility.

Before I left England my mother mentioned to me that the son of her best friend in Ireland, Denis Freeman was a Captain working undercover somewhere in Asia Minor, i.e. Jordan, Irak or Syria and Lebanon. Back to the hot springs. I heard the engine of a vehicle in the distance and loosed off a couple of shots. When the headlights appeared on the causeway I fired in the air again. It stopped and I shouted. Relief was colossal. Saved! As I thanked them profusely, one of them said to the other: 'Something, something, Denis...' I said, 'Freeman?' It was! The most incredible coincidence of my life.

On the same trip we went to see Kerak crusader castle. Much of it was still standing. I discovered a well with steps descending. I borrowed a torch and descended the mossy and slimy steps for some hundred feet or more. Conditions were getting worse but I just had to get to the bottom. The torch was fading fast. Clearly I was the first idiot to descend so far for many years, for at the bottom I found a battered copy of the Koran and an old musket, both of which I took back to camp. I have often wondered how they had reached a few feet above the water line. Getting up the slimy steps in the dark was quite a feat. I saw a similar musket on the Antiques Road Show recently valued at twelve thousand pounds and on leaving the regiment I had given it away. Oh dear!

Near the end of our stay in Aqaba, Colonel Charles asked me if I would like to stay on as a regular in the regiment. This was a great honour for a National Serviceman and had I known of how army pay would soar, I would have stayed, and might have become a general, as my aunt Alice had foretold, but such was my boredom with no wars to fight and little to do, plus struggling to exist on my army pay, that I made the mistake of a lifetime, which I have frequently regretted and I turned the offer down. We did have three generals in my family tree so it was not unheard of and the inefficiency of certain officers and their lack of imagination reduced the competition. My proficiency in Chess and expertise in the board game, L'attaque were surely signs of potential!

So I set off by troop ship with the advance guard to Cyprus, except I was getting off at Port Said, to fly home to Blackbush airport. I was asked to keep an eye on the horses, but the troopers looked after them well enough.

Forgotten Soldiers

They taught us how to fight
We walked all through the night
They taught us many ways to kill
We sweltered on the sand
In many foreign lands
But we longed for our homeland still.

We were young and neat
Now you pass us on the street
We are the forgotten soldiers.
Brother got a bite to eat?
Old shoes for my bleeding feet?
We're the forgotten soldiers.

Under terrorist attack
We would watch your back
We were the heroes then.
In earthquake, fire or flood
We searched through stinking mud
We were the welcome men.

Remember pretty girls?
Their eyes would gleam like pearls
As uniforms went marching by.
We'd lie there in the dusk
All that's left, a husk
Enough to make a proud man cry.

You look at us like scum,
Remember my old mum?
Proudly watching us march away.
When war was safely past
They brought us back at last.
No, don't look the other way!

Remember Harry – Tom?
He defused the bomb
They found behind the station.
He's proudly picking litter
No wonder he's so bitter
Forgotten by the bleeding nation.

(My Protest Poem!)

23

Civilian Life

RETURNING TO ENGLAND I went by train to see my parents and helped on the farm for a few days as Mother was ill. While in Jordan I had corresponded with a school friend, Richard Barder's dad. He was Chairman of The National Fur Company in Knightsbridge, just down the road from Harrods, before that Egyptian took it over. He said he would try to find me a job in London. Meantime I was broke. I had just enough cash to get to London and find myself some digs in the last part of Kensington before it deteriorates into Earls Court, now a cheap home to half the Australian nation.

In those days the army used you and dumped you. No care as to what happened after you left. No counselling. Just, 'Goodbye'. Certainly there was no financial support. Still just twenty, with no training apart from farming and soldiering, and little experience of civilian life, I was at a loss as what to do and hoped that Richard's dad would come up trumps.

Later, being in the Territorial army for the next three years, in the Shropshire Yeomanry, one had ones travel paid and a generous payment for a long weekend four times a year. We would drive round the Shropshire lanes, trying not to get lost. I would stop my scout car outside a pub come mid-day and report in to base: 'My batteries are fa-ading' as I treated my crew to a pint.

Our colonel, Lord Cavan, kindly said that he would put my name forward for the Cavalry Club. The entry fee was twenty five pounds or two and a half week's wages so I gratefully declined. In retrospect it was not the best thing to do. I might have met all sorts of influential people there, and have found a really worthwhile job. Hindsight!

I found a job washing cars. Not very becoming for an ex Queens Bays officer? It kept me housed and fed. Clean and quite well paid but cool in freezing February. Lord Grey, whom I had met in the Cavalry, did not recognise me as I returned his car but he gave me a generous tip of two shillings and six pence, enough for two meals in a café I frequented.

London had not been cleaned up in 1956 and thick fogs occurred occasionally. The worst in broad daylight was so thick that I could not see the edge of the pavement on my bike so I wheeled it along carefully off the road.

I saw the headlights of a bus at about five metres distance, creeping on its way and little other traffic ventured out. On clear days traffic was not nearly as heavy as now and some cars were driving down Park Lane at over forty miles an hour. During rush hour I was nearly sandwiched between two double-decker buses. You just had to stop and let them by.

The Chelsea Arts Ball still took place annually. Six leading jazz bands including Kenny Ball, Ivy Benson, Ken Collier and Chris Barber were present. It was a great occasion with everyone going in fancy dress, all six thousand young people. Vinyl records from those times fetch good prices nowadays. Don't throw them away till you have checked their price on the Net.

I was staying in quite a smart guest house alongside Admirals' widows, who treated me like a stray dog and brought me back chicken's legs and the like from where one of them was a cook in a smart restaurant; so kind. The cost of the guest house was too much and I found a broom cupboard to live in for a couple of months. It had no window, just room for the bed and to change ones clothes plus a chair to put them on. My worldly possessions were in Wales, sent there by the army, so I needed little room. Just as well. Aged just twenty, one can rough it for a while.

Suddenly I received an invitation to an interview from Berliners, a whole-sale furriers, friends of the Barders. Phillip Berliner, an ex- army major in the war, was friendly and had a twinkle in his eye. His older brother, Harold, was a little remote. Their partner and salesman, Mr Turnham, was friendly even though as a trainee salesman, perhaps I was the future opposition? I got the job on ten pounds a week; just enough to survive on in London at that time.

I bought a decent suit on the 'never-never' and found digs near Queensway, in Westbourne Gardens, round the corner from the Turkish Baths. The digs cost me one pound, thirty five a week and I had a basement room looking out onto a little garden, and shared a bathroom, which only I seemed to use, with a retired Admiral, whom I hardly ever met. Perhaps he was a ghost! It was ideally situated only ten minutes by tube from Oxford Circus, a few hundred yards from Berliners in Margaret Street. My landlord, Mr Smith, was a saxophone player in the Victoria Palace Theatre, hosting the Goon Show. Later he was to give me two lessons to launch my sax career. I found it cheaper to go out to the pictures rather than sit at home during winter months, feeding the gas meter.

Work in a furriers is seasonal, correlated with the cold weather. I was first to work in the skin room, where freshly treated mink, ermine, musquash and squirrel were sorted into matching bundles, prior to being fashioned into coats or capes with the odd stole. Ermine is very expensive and a coat of sapphire mink, which are bred on farms, would have paid for a decent house at that time. Mink are vicious little animals similar to the stoat and when some escaped in Norfolk, they became a real pest raiding chicken houses. Fred Kingston was my tutor there, with an emphasis on what constituted quality skins. Some were to end up on film stars' backs as we only dealt with the cream of the market, Dickens and Jones, Harrods and the like. Fred was a kindly and intelligent fellow with one son of whom he was very proud.

After a few months in the skin room, I was moved to the workshop where about sixteen men stretched the skins, pegged out with nails, fashioned to patterns and sewed into fashionable garments. Everyone was friendly and I gravitated round the room hearing gossip and even reminiscences of one who had been a 'guest' of the Japs during the war. Charlie was in charge and the hub of the workshop, obviously respected by all as their immediate boss.

Some time later, I joined the two girls in the office upstairs and waited for the season to start. The two Marys were very friendly and pleasant but the inactivity was hard to bear. I asked Mr Philip as he was known, to give me something to do but apart from Mr Turnham giving me a few hints as how to sell the furs round the shops, life was not madly exciting. So much that I would blatantly read a book in the office much of the time. In the corner, glued to his work but occasionally giving me hostile glances, sat the grey little accountant. He was such a nonentity that it clean put me off accountancy.

24

Friends in London

SOON I MET a kindred spirit, Jonathan Wren, I can't remember how. It was 1956. He lived in a basement near Leicester Square with two smelly Siamese cats. He never seemed to have any girl friends or boy friends. Totally sexless? He loved the theatre and was madly generous, even when he could not afford to be. He once took several acquaintances, including me to 'The Talk of the Town', where one has a very nice dinner prior to watching the theatre. He took an old lady to the theatre when he had only just met her in the street. He was eccentric but with a heart of gold. He worked at night in a coffee bar where most of the waiters were gay, as the washer-up in the basement and got me a job there twice a week in the evenings doing the same. When we worked together some nights, he would toss me a cup to dry, careless of its direction and the breakages were frequent.

Sadly John opened a specialist "Banks only" employment agency in the Strand, a smart address if only in a little top storey flat. He had no idea of book keeping and failed to keep any records. Thus spending out-stripped income very fast. I went over to see if I could organise things for him and found three bin liners full of bills and very few receipts. He was up to his neck in trouble. He took an overdose but the pills he had been taking overcame the sleeping pills and he woke up feeling fine. A few weeks later he committed suicide more efficiently, and that was the end of a generous, eccentric friend. I hope someone cared for the cats. An Armenian Jew took over his business and made it a roaring success. Ironic!

Speaking of Jews, I met a girl with very long hair and a slightly wild expression, through John Wren. She was "arty" and seemed a fast mover. At only our second meeting she wanted to introduce me to her parents and we had not reached an even slightly romantic stage. I was not vaguely attracted to her and when we reached her opulent home I stopped at her gate and making some excuse, accelerated down the street. I wonder whether she ever snared a partner, poor chap?

Reverting to the café, trays full of cups would descend the lift for us to lift into the washing machine at an alarming rate and saucepans to be scoured as food was also served. When the theatres closed, a mob of people would arrive, all expecting to be served at once.

One evening a homosexual waited till I was on my own and made advances to me. I threatened him with my godfather judge and the chief of the Metropolitan Police, who was his friend and the man retreated. He was a member of the Royal Ballet and they are pretty tough as John Wren's brother Walter discovered when he punched one. Walter boxed for the Royal Navy but it was he who picked himself up out of the gutter.

During our hour long lunch breaks I would go up to Regents Park to lounge on the grass and enjoy the wonderful Nash terraces on the way. Sometimes beer was being delivered to a pub by the old-fashioned Suffolk Punch horses with all their leather and brass trappings and furry hooves; a fine sight. They pulled a four wheeler cart as they would have done a hundred years before. In Hyde Park, close to Bayswater Terrace where my mother was born, the pavement artists worked. They were so skilled it seemed a shame they could not draw with their many coloured chalks on paper and sell their art. Smartly dressed women would ride along Rotten Row, looking down their haughty noses at us common people. I wondered what their day jobs might be, Prostitutes?

On the proceeds of working in the coffee bar I was able to visit Brussels over one Easter and enjoyed the night club with its jazz under the steps of the bank in La Grande Place. I also visited Ghent, which had come through the war pretty well. It has wonderful roofs you can see from a cathedral tower. They looked like a fairy tale, completely uneven and unique, orange, brown, or red. Another Easter I stayed with a friend's family in Amsterdam and visited the Keukenhof with its gorgeous tulips. In those days it was a clean and safe city without drug and immigration problems and the fear of losing its national identity.

To pay for the next trip I painted the flat of an eccentric friend of my mother's, Audrey Henson. She was a respected eye specialist in Stafford Street, just off Bond Street. One day while I was stretched balancing precariously over the three storey stairs, painting, a film star came up them for an appointment. Audrey had three cats, which kept to the roof garden most times. She was also friends with the famous Olympic runner, Jim Peters. When I met him there, he had put on many pounds in weight. He was the man who was far in front in the Marathon in the Commonwealth Games in 1954 and then he collapsed just a few yards short of the finishing line. He was very pleasant and friendly.

25

Moscow 1957

MY BEST TRIP abroad resulting from Audrey Henson's friendship, was a trip to Moscow. Like John Wren, she was always on the side of the underdogs, who at that time were the communists. She gave me the details of a trip to Moscow. It was ostensibly for young Communists from all over the world and I told Audrey I was a true blue Tory. She said: 'Keep quiet about that. It's a trip of a lifetime.' One has to remember it was the height of the Cold War and my employers thought me mad to entertain the thought of such a trip for an ex British army officer, knowledgeable about the latest self-levelling tank gun. The Hungarian revolution was still rumbling and our train had to pass through the tip of Hungary. They said they would never see me again, but I thought it worth the risk. The trip included travel by air to Prague, food and a free ticket to the Bolshoi Ballet at the Moscow Dynamo Stadium, illuminated by searchlights.

In Prague, where we spent one night, everything seemed cold and grey including the buildings. Somehow I got invited out by some students and was shown around their theatre. They gave me cherry brandy, a great luxury. How is it that all this happens to me? God knows. One criterion for this is to talk with anyone, to show interest in them and what they do, to be ready to join in activities, which was safer in those days. If you just sit back and hope things will happen, they won't.

We stopped at one station in Russia to be met by the usual friendly crowd. They had never seen a black man before and surrounded one of our passengers before throwing him up in the air like a doll. Unfortunately they failed to catch him, so he landed heavily.

We had tickets to the Bolshoi Theatre to see Eugene Onegin. Great for realism, they had a real fire burning on the huge stage – you could feel the heat – and four horses drawing a carriage. It was a wonderful evening. We also had tickets for dining at the Moscow equivalent of the Hilton Hotel and having teamed up with a Russian interpreter in the Royal Navy, we went there for dinner. We had finished a heavy but pleasant meal when we were hailed by a group of four Ruskies. They insisted we join them for another meal. Stuffing ourselves was one thing but keeping up with their incessant demands for vodka was something else. They would not take no for an answer and as soon as one set of glasses was empty, they ordered another. Very hospitable but I was told next morning I danced all the way home on the underground railway, the Metro.

The Metro or underground railway system is like a palace. It has marble columns and beautiful wall sculptures and mosaics depicting past historical triumphs, such as the defeat of Napoleon. There was not a trace of litter. Trains moved on time and smoothly.

Moscow in those days seemed a very bleak city with unimaginative architecture and grey concrete buildings everywhere. The main streets were well planned for the future with eight lanes in each direction. There was hardly any traffic, so it seemed incongruous. Occasionally an important person would pass by in a large black car with motor cycle outriders. The populace were totally brainwashed into thinking the free West had strikes broken up with riot forces with machine guns. They just laughed when one denied this and dismissed it as propaganda. Yet they were pathetically interested in the outside world, if one could get them away from the 'grey men' KGB stooges and on their own.

When Russian children were born, they were whisked away to foster parents immediately. There was no family life. They were brought up in mass kindergartens and schools. If a child wanted to be a farmer but had shown a natural gift in Chemistry, he would have to become a chemist if they were in short supply.

We stayed in hostels, single room barrack like accommodation with tough looking Russian women guarding each floor. I would not like to have tangled with one of them! If one tried to talk to locals, very soon a grey looking figure would appear and the crowd around us would evaporate. The KGB were everywhere, it seemed.

The next day my naval friend and I set off for the railway station, against express instructions not to leave Moscow. How could they trail every one of the thousands of young communists imported from all over the world?

We boarded a train and disembarked at a distant village. Here we had a meal of typical greasy vegetable soup with the odd blob of chewy meat floating in it. The free meal tickets we had been given in Moscow were honoured out in the country villages. The beer cart, a huge barrel on wheels pulled by a pony, arrived and we tasted the beer, which was vinegary. You would have to be pretty desperate to drink it, but presumably the locals did.

There were a few shops selling basic groceries and even films to replenish our cameras. The street opened out into the countryside and we found children seated round a haystack. Two women were loading hay with pitch-forks onto a horse driven cart. They ignored our presence. Our clothes gave us away as foreigners.

Houses were all wooden cabins built of horizontal rough logs. They shared one outside stand pipe for water between four cabins. The loos were outside too. Just imagine getting up in the middle of the night in mid-winter. They can have over thirty degrees of frost there. The local church was boarded up, surrounded by litter and obviously not used. However churches in Moscow were very well attended, a silent challenge to their communist masters. Since the end of the Cold War, Religion has experienced a huge surge upwards.

We were suddenly surrounded by men in uniform and hustled down to the station to await the next train. They told us grimly to go straight back to Moscow so we got off at the next station. It's a wonder we avoided prison. Another Briton had his camera confiscated and was fined for taking photos unwittingly near an army area. We found the next village a replica of the first with nothing of particular interest so we took the first train to Moscow.

On our return we found a note inviting us and about another fifty especially selected British to a cocktail party at our embassy. As we circulated we were warned to be careful what we said as the place was bugged by the Russians. We also realized that out of the thousand or so British at the Young Communists Youth Festival, all our party were actually anti-communist. Just how had the Intelligence fathomed who to invite? Makes your flesh creep!

26

Return to London Town

ON THE TRAIN back to Prague I caught Asian flu. How fitting! All my bones ached unmercifully and I had a temperature of 105. Yes, pretty ill. One of the train's wooden seats was cleared and a British nurse cared for me. I survived and once back in London was greeted by a Daily Express reporter. I had been mentioned in a local paper as having said something derogatory about Moscow. Anyhow she paid for us to have a very good lunch and I refused to say anything anti- Russian. How the vultures prey!

John Wren and I cycled miles into the country, staying at youth hostels and visited Lord Montague's car exhibition at Beaulieu. They had Sir Malcolm Campbell's world record breaker, Bluebird there and a host of wonderful old vehicles. This is where most of the period films hire their cars from. They must have a very competent workshop as just imagine how modern actors would change gear trying to double de-clutch!

How much ones clothes matter in how others assess you. I was amused to be greeted by cinema concierges in totally different ways. If I wore my ex cavalry British Warm, a very smart overcoat, it was "this way Sir, that Sir." If I entered in a sweater and ordinary trousers, it was" "Over there, lad." There is a message for us all there.

I played rugby for a minor club, The Port of London Authority and was in a pub after a match talking about our game with two friends when a little man came up to us and said: 'Don't go away. I'll be back soon.' We looked at each other in wonder and sank another pint or two. Soon he appeared with a soccer ball for Fred the soccer player and two rugby balls for Andrew and myself. They were brand new, had never been blown up and Gilberts, the make that the world internationals are still played with. Apart from plying him with beer, what could we do! I imagine they must have 'fallen off the back of a lorry', but it was both kind and incredible.

My wonderful Aunt Alice gave me a beautiful concertina in a fabulous shiny box. It looked as if it had never been played. I tried but it was not the instrument for me. While at Marlborough I stopped wasting my parents' money on piano lessons as I never practised and the patient teacher eventually told me I was not musical. I did however conquer the bugle and played it with gusto as we marched down Marlborough's high street in the CCF band. The concertina was used as a down payment at Boosey and Hawkes for a Tenor Saxophone.

As members of the Combined Cadet Force, we went on a summer camp on Salisbury plain where I managed to damage my Achilles tendon, which saved me from further route marches; not very thrilling pass-times. One evening there were many hundreds of boys from Marlborough and other schools all aged sixteen in a huge NAAFI tent and quite a hubbub as might be expected. David Hunt, one of the Marlborough fraternity, opened up the piano and the magic of his playing quietened everyone till you could hear a pin drop. It must be wonderful to have such a touch and the expertise.

After Mr Smith showing me where the notes were and giving me some sound advice, I was soon playing tunes after a fashion in the Royal Oak pub, near Paddington. The pub was opposite the police station. Around ten o'clock every night I would pack up my beloved instrument, ducking from the occasional flying chair as the regular fights started up. Earlier they were too drunk to notice the odd wrong note, so what better place to learn? The non-musical lad was launched. It was a calculated risk playing there. One night as I left the pub, sax case in hand, I passed a man waiting outside, blood streaming from his face, and holding an open cut-throat razor, presumably ready for his adversary. I did not hang around to see what happened. Recently an Irish friend told me it was the roughest pub in London. I won't argue with that!

Eventually the selling season was upon us and I was lent a hired van with which to tour southern England, selling furs. I had never driven in London's mad traffic and during the first day was too slow to avoid a bus pulling out with no signal. Returning to base with a sixty pound bill for my bent front bumper, I was not popular. With the van repaired, I was given six driving lessons paid for by the Berliners. I had never taken a test in my life. As regimental MTO, I had given myself a pink slip saying I could drive. I had to test my own drivers so why not myself! Unfortunately London was a little different from the road between Aqaba and Ma'an.

The firm soon got its money back as I opened a thriving account with Bentalls, a smart store in Surrey. I gained sixty pounds commission in a month, mostly due to the buyer there, a lady of advanced years, with a glass eye, who took a shine to me. I refused the invitation to go to the theatre with her but she still clearly lived in hope and the orders flowed in.

London has always been a lonely place unless one has money. I had a girl-friend for a while, a pretty young nurse but we split after some weeks. Not much in common. I would take long walks at night to keep fit and wandered into the Queensway library looking for career inspiration. I did manage to afford a visit to Humphrey Lyttleton's jazz club at 101, Oxford Street. I soon appreciated why this was one of the institutions of London town. What wonderful sounds and rhythms. Ronnie Scott's in Leicester Square was another attraction.

At one stage of the year Soho has a wild Carnival. I can't think how I got up there, but an ex school friend recognized me while on top of a tele-phone box. On another occasion another recognized me by my unique walk in Piccadilly late one night. He told me that our old housemaster, George Tarleton was dying in hospital. To my regret I never went to see him.

I could not imagine staying in the fur trade, which even in 1956 was on the decline. I lacked a mentor with the experience, who could have pointed me in the right direction, whatever that might have been. I eventually went to a school friend's party and Simon's dad learnt that I was bored with the fur trade. He suggested that he could get a friend in New Zealand to find a job for me over there. He kept his word and before long I was offered a job work-ing on a sheep station with the Bamfords in windy Wairarapa, North Island.

27

New Zealand

THE TRIP TO New Zealand on one of the New Zealand shipping company's ships, the fourteen thousand ton Rangitane, took six weeks to convey its four hundred passengers half way round the world. We passed through the Panama canal where the contrast between rich and poor was terrible. The latter lived in shacks made of corrugated iron with walls covered with newspapers. The churches looked ornate and very rich. Would Jesus have approved?

I played a lot of pontoon and made enough money to pay for my drinks all the way. You pretend to have a mannerism like a twitch when you have a bad hand and then take opponents to the cleaners when you get a good hand. I also was runner up for the Chess prize, having beaten the winner several times previously. Over confident?

Food on board was excellent and on one stormy breakfast time, only four of us appeared for the meal. The port holes were rapidly closed as the sea invaded us spurting across the room. We had plenty of choice and much laughter as the plates slid from one side of the table to the other with every wave. I have never suffered from sea sickness, even when all hatches were battened down and we were lurching all over the place, as I treat it like a free funfair ride. All in the mind! Considering the trip was only ten pounds for those of us that were going to certain occupations, deer cullers, herd testers and farm workers, it was very good value to be "a ten pound pom."

Arriving at Wellington, windy as usual, I took a train up to Masterton and was met by my employer, Ron Bamford. He took me into a shop and got me to buy waterproof leggings and an oil skin coat and hat, invaluable when going round the lambs on horseback in a storm. Masterton was a one horse town. I.E. It only had one street of shops. The pubs had long bars and not much else. Outside were rails to which you could tie your horse. We soon left for Ron's sheep station forty miles out on the coast in his car.

I was shown into my new home, a hut at the bottom of the garden. It was private and crowned by a fruit tree. When the nectarines disappeared, I blamed the possums. I ate with the family, Ron, his wife and twelve year old son, Alan plus older son, Derek, aged about twenty. Mrs Doris Bamford was used to having a younger 'boy about the place' and treated me accordingly. I was amused when she showed an ex cavalry officer how to use a table napkin.

The sheep station was comparatively small, three thousand acres, when compared with Homewood next door, ten thousand acres owned by Fred Tatham, Ron's brother-in law. Ron kept eight sheep per acre on the rich flat land bordered by the sea. This contrasts with thirty acres per sheep in much of Australia. In the rolling foot hills he had beef cattle, which kept the grass down short enough for sheep. Much of it was covered by native bush, manuka growing up to about fifteen feet in height. They engaged the Thomson brothers to smash down the bush with their dozer blades. Sometimes it was so steep, they were virtually riding down on their blades. They had a huge iron ball on a chain between the two dozers and it flattened anything in its way. When squashed down, the bush burnt well. In three weeks' time, when cool, the land was sown with grass seeds and fertilizer by air and after another six weeks it would be covered in grass. To increase the fertility, Michael Bamford, the elder son, packed sheep onto the newly grassed slopes at night so they would give it the best fertilizer in the world. It was a pretty neat idea.

Squeamish? Miss this Paragraph.

My first job was to milk the house cow every morning, which meant getting up in all weathers at six, and so I put an end to that one by never quite milking her out, which caused her to dry off much sooner than she should have, so milk would come out twice a week on the mail bus from Masterton. The job I detested was catching a sheep from the holding paddock and cutting its throat, before skinning it. It was best in that order! One had to cut, break its neck and cut again, which I reckoned to do in one second. To kill and skin the sheep, gutting it and hanging it up on the hooks took me four minutes fifteen seconds, after a bit of practice.

A Life Insurance salesman would come and collect the hardened fat from the sheep, which presumably he sold to be made into soap. A nice little earner on the side. The offal would go to the dogs having been boiled to kill any Hydatids germs, a deadly disease hibernating in the liver. The four of us, if Alan was away at boarding school, plus Michael and his wife, April, got through one fully grown sheep a week. The couple lived about a quarter of a mile away, in a modern house with a huge plate glass window facing the sea. When the notorious Wairarapa wind blew, the glass would bend.

I helped Michael add a garage. We laid the concrete base and then put up wooden walls. We laid on electricity and a water tap. Living out in the country, farmers have to be their own tradesmen plus vets – self-sufficient.

Like my father, he planted vegetable seeds at the end of a crop. Electricity was generated by a windmill attached to twelve car batteries. We were never short, as Wairarapa is known for its wind. It can be so strong that the sheep all mount up on each other at the end of a paddock and we had to cut the fence wires to stop them suffocating.

Pheasants bred well in the nearby woods. A member of the family would soak barley in whisky and then scatter the grain along the fence where the pheasants congregated at sundown. The pheasants ate the grain and then sat on the fence till the alcohol took over. They would fall to the ground, drunk and it was simple to collect them for the deep freezer.

Sheep can be madly hysterical when another sheep goes off with their lambs. They run round in circles baaing and have a real difficulty in recognizing their own lambs. Some sheep, yet to lamb, will "lambnap" another's lamb. When they lamb themselves, confusion sets in and they may reject the first one. To get a ewe to take on a motherless lamb, I would skin the ewe's dead lamb and fit the skin over the "changeling". Then I would bale up the ewe till its new lamb was sucking from it. This method worked almost every time. Another risk with sheep is the Maori dog, often left to roam. One morning we found one hundred and twenty sheep mauled or killed by dogs. We carried rifles in our saddle holsters after that and shot three of the dogs. That stopped their worrying.

28

Local Characters

I GOT ON well with the local Maoris and went pig hunting with Phil Pucu. I carried my .303 rifle and he just used a knife. His dogs would bale up the wild pig and he would dart in with his knife, seize a hind leg, flip it on its back and kill it. The dogs had to be quick and brave as the boars could slit them open as one did to Phil after I had left the country. His life was only just saved as he dragged himself back to their homestead and he was driven the forty miles into Masterton to hospital. The Pucus held a hangi, a feast, which went on for days and to which I was invited. I brought a dozen of beer and retreated when they had been drunk.

On the next door sheep station they had six cadets, eighteen year-olds from Hawkes Bay gaining experience in similar country but away from their dads. They learnt new farming techniques and responsibility. I quickly made friends with them, a thoroughly pleasant group. The tall Bill Shaw, son of an All Black, taught me how to develop, enlarge and print black and white photos. He was a tower of strength when hay making and could toss a heavy bale right up to the top of the barn.

John Todd became a close friend and still is. He would drive me in to town, before I bought my big black Standard Vanguard, and we were frequently on two wheels, or just sliding round the loose metal road corners. A wonder we lived. Michael Oliver, aged eighteen, who worked for Michael Moore on the next property towards Masterton, also drove like a madman, and in spite of my warning, went through his windscreen. He lived but he had to have a replacement windscreen plus some time in hospital.

Paddy White, one of Michael Moore's cadets, used to spin his van one and a half rotations. On loose metal roads it was possible. Anne, Michael Moore's sister, was coming home one night when a wild pig got in her way. They are very solid and she spent six weeks in hospital.

Michael used to have some wild parties. One dark night we had to tow a Land-Rover from a bridge because the nearside wheels were over the edge. On another occasion Michael was in a friend's house. When the phone went, he dragged phone and fitting off the wall and handed it to the house owner in the next room. I hope you won't mind my passing that on, Michael. We were a wild bunch.

In his own house Michael had a gramophone speaker set in the ceiling so the sound filled the room and it had a marvellous effect. A wonder more people do not try it.

Bill was a bit of a 'dag' or a card, as Victorians used to say. He was very clever mechanically and shortened his model T Ford truck so if he lent back in the seat, it would do a 'wheelie'. After a bit he kept a hook and chain on the truck to pull astonished drivers out of the ditch. Bill once gave the local police something to think about when he marched into the Masterton police station and deposited a skull on the desk. It was probably from an uncovered Maori grave on the sea shore.

At weekends we would play rugby, or coarse rugby. It was fairly brutal as I soon discovered. I tried to tackle an ox like player, thinking he must surely side-step me at the last moment. No. He kept coming, his head lowered right into my solar plexus. He ran through for a try and I lay unattended for some time, seriously winded. After the match we would all get a skin-full of beer and one night I drove home rather the worse for wear. At the end of the drive, one headlight pointed upward and the other down. Luckily there was a full moon. I lent the car to Roddy Rutherford on the understanding that if he had it repaired, he could borrow it for a year and then sell it and give me the proceeds. This worked rather well.

I made friends with an English couple, who had a bit of land close to us. They invited me over for a meal and drinks and on the way back, in pitch blackness I let the horse have loose reins and he found the way home with no trouble.

My main jobs were to ride round the sheep in all weathers checking they were not cast, rolled over on their backs, their legs in the air, helpless and so fat that they could not right themselves. Also, the sheep being an intelligent animal, will lamb over the edge of a creek if it possibly can. So I had to search the creek edges to see how many lambs I could resuscitate or bring up the bank before they fell into the water. I would have to help some sheep lamb as they had difficulties. Unfortunately I have fair sized hands so it must have been a painful experience for many. I would have to wash in Dettol first and then give them a shot of penicillin to prevent any blood poisoning, which otherwise would usually kill the ewe.

Michael Bamford had a red coloured dog without a brain in its head. I often wondered why he kept it. One day we were driving along in the model

T and crossing the deep ditch over the bridge. This dog was running along-side of us, happily barking up at us so it never saw the ditch till it was somer-saulting into the water at the bottom. Laugh!

We eventually went round the sheep with a motorbike and side car. The latter was useful for carrying back a sick sheep but from a lower viewpoint, one could not see the sheep so well as from up on a horse. In a sixty or hundred acre paddock, there is a fair old territory to cover. One day the wind was so strong, I opened a gate, drove through on the bike, got off it to shut the gate and the wind blew it back through the opening before I could shut it. After two abortive attempts, I parked the bike and side car parallel to the gate.

We used to go over to the Tathams for tennis but I gave up after being told off for hitting the ball too hard. If I hit it softly, it would always drive into the net. Another enjoyable pastime was searching for crayfish, similar to the best of British lobsters. We would wait for a wave to crash into the rocks, hold our breath and dive down under the rocks to where the crays were lurking. Grabbing a cray in both hands, we waited till the next wave had crashed and then catapulted off the bottom to the surface and safety before another wave arrived.

There was a farmer a few miles along from us called Meredith. I don't know why but there seemed to be bad blood between the Merediths and the other locals. Their land ran down to the sea too and one Christmas we were down on the beach when a top dressing plane buzzed us. We ran out of the way and it landed safely on the beach. No one got out so after a while some-one went over and opened the door. The pilot, one of the Thorne brothers, fell out, stone drunk. That is how he had been flying. Those were the days!

Drink was a problem in society across the board. If you went to a race meeting, you always had a dozen of home brew in your car boot. The bottles were twice the size of present day ones. It was fairly lethal but probably compensated for losing your shirt on slow horses.

We would make top quality clover and lucerne hay to sell to race horse owners. One could get two or even three crops a year and it would dry in a day to a beautiful blue colour. The baler left it in neat rows and then a low deck large lorry with a side loader would drive along and an endless stream of bales would arrive to be stacked on the lorry. It was efficient but very hard work stacking the bales.

Our sheep were either Southdown for meat alone; they grow virtually no wool. Or there were Romney/Leicester crosses, which produced eight pounds of good quality wool. They were susceptible to wool blindness, where the Romney influence caused the wool to grow into their eyes. So we had to wig them, clearing their eyes, and dag them, which meant cleaning up round their back sides before lambing so there were no obstructions. It was back breaking work. I watched Johnny Morris set a new record, shearing three hundred and eighty sheep in eight hours. He later toured England demonstrating the art.

Fencing was another task. Fences were seven wires, the top being barbed and getting closer together as they neared the ground. Each end of a stretch of fence would be anchored with a concrete strainer, itself anchored at its foot buried three feet down. The wires were threaded through concrete posts so if an angry bull charged, the fence would give way as the wires stretched and then catapult the bull back where he had come from. A cartoon here please! So no fence posts would break.

The creek was full of healthy looking watercress, delicious in salad, but the Bamfords were not game to eat it in case a dead sheep was further up the creek. We had wonderful and delicious asparagus. It grew so well because they had buried a dead horse under it. Nice!

Communication was by the party line phone, so constructed that if you wanted to ring someone, you wound a handle. Then all the busybodies in the district would run to their phones and listen in. It was an ideal opportunity to feed false information.

We eventually would fly into Masterton in Michael Bamford's Cessna. We built a hanger to protect it from the wind, using large posts joined with wire, and threaded bush between dual wires. It worked well. After I had left New Zealand, a silly Englishman borrowed the plane and crashed it in the foothills, killing himself, flying too low and disobeying the warning of down-draughts.

Michael Bamford was always seeking ways to improve the property's finances. Sadly he started planting fruit trees in this super sheep country and they did not do well. He died of cancer quite young. We had got on well enough together. He had also been in the army for a short time, which probably helped. Derek was a bit remote and not over friendly. I am told he went to live in South Island, having also married. Young Alan, who never seemed to speak, and ran away from school, I never caught up with. Perhaps he is Minister for Education!

Ron Bamford retired soon after I left the country and only lived a couple of years longer. He had come out to New Zealand as a young man from the UK and worked hard all his life. A shame he could not have lived longer to enjoy a well-deserved rest. He once told me off for entering the house from the front door. As a mere worker, it was the tradesman's entrance for me! I can just imagine my haughty cousin, Susan Lumley, meeting Ron. 'What a common little man!' she would say. John Cleese had it right in Fawlty Towers!

Local people were incredibly friendly and hospitable. The Camerons of Glendhu asked me to stay on their remote property. There was no road there. I walked my horse through the river and stayed a day or two. On my return it had rained and the river had risen so it was now about seventy yards across and flowing fast. I swam my horse back, perched precariously on its back and hardly got wet. A great horse that one. If we were rounding up cattle, it would see one break from the mob before I did and turn on a sixpence to head it back. It would have made a champion polo pony.

New Zealand sheep farming was an interesting experience and probably honed my character. At least I was never bored. I bought my first typewriter there, paying for it with possum skins and mushrooms, which went into town on the mail bus. The government paid two shillings and six pence for each strip off the back. The possum was a real pest, ruining fruit trees and others. And competing with me for my nectarines!

29

Taranaki

AFTER EIGHTEEN MONTHS of working for the Bamfords, I wanted something more interesting and applied for a job as a herd tester in Taranaki. I got permission easily from the government to leave my job as Herd Testers were in short supply, and headed north to Hawkes Bay to pick peaches for three weeks. We were allowed to eat as many as we liked. In their cunning way, they knew this was the quickest method of curing any desire for peaches for a long time, but I ate little else for the first two days. We stayed in little wooden shacks and the money was good.

Next stop, Inglewood, near New Plymouth. Taranaki is virtually entirely dairy farming and our testing was for the butter fat in the milk. It surrounds Mount Egmont, as it used to be known. The mountain should be treated with respect by climbers. One year seven nurses fell to their deaths roped together.

Kind farmer's wives would do my washing for me and everything would be beautifully ironed. One fooled about with my precious saxophone and there was nearly an international incident when she broke the reed. Reeds are terribly brittle and it was easily done. You have to go through a box of reeds before you find one with the right tight and uniform grain. They should last for many months with due care.

One stayed each night at the farm you were testing and some of the farmers gave up their best room for the tester. Not always. I had to share the chicken shed with the sixteen year old son where they had eleven sons and no daughters. It was bitterly cold in winter and blankets were in short supply. At least there were no chickens!

I had joined the new band, the Daltones, where at twenty three, I was the grand old man out of ten players. I would get back from playing about one thirty in the morning and had to be up for milking at a quarter to four. So at least there was only a short time to shiver in bed.

That same farmer asked me if I would go down his well to clean it out. None of his family was game. The well was not cased and having been winched down in a bucket to the bottom some thirty feet below, the odd clod of earth would descend on me. It was hot up top and very cold down there. I cleaned it out and was hoisted up again. My fears of being left down there vanished as I thought of the water becoming foul for a long time! Having spent a very unpleasant hour or so down there, the farmer was furious when I claimed double time as danger money but he paid up with bad grace in the end. I helped him get his hay in, which started a lifetime battle with hay fever.

On returning to the UK, I was tested in Wimpole Street , next to Harley Street where all the top experts are said to work, and was allergic to eighty out of eighty tests. The specialist said: "You poor fellow". I was to discover just how poor.

One task I took on was to help a farmer with removing tree stumps from his marshy paddock, prior to draining it and making it into good pasture. We drilled holes in the massive stumps and placed plastic explosive in them. Then we tested the roll of fuse for speed as it is best not to blow oneself up as well. Then we lit the fuse and walked quickly away. You never run in case of tripping and being blown apart. The stumps flew fifty feet or more into the air and descended in little pieces. Quite a spectacle. On one of these occasions a top dressing pilot was working nearby when he spotted us. I got my camera out and took a picture of him dive bombing me. I fell over on my back, which was just as well as he passed over me at about five feet above land, so I would have lost my head. Not to be encouraged. Yes, they are a mad lot!

High-flying Moments!
Plane at five feet – I'm almost six feet!

On the hill above the marsh a farmer was working three huge horses pulling a harrow. He was following the contours as it was too steep to take a tractor. I took a photo of the horses, where one could see over the top of one horse and under the belly of the next. Yes it was steep. And I received half a week's wages from the Auckland Weekly News, the leading New Zealand magazine for the photo. Very gratifying.

The Daltones band was managed by George Preece, a hypnotist. He did things very well. We practiced for hours on end and did not stop till our recording sounded very like Billy Vaughan, the leading Australian band at that time. We played at Waitara town hall every weekend and had over twelve hundred dancers most nights. George laid on prizes for statue dances and the like and I guess we must have been pretty good as the band went on for over twenty five years with a name change or two. During the week we split up and played at the many village halls. I was making more money from music than from herd testing. My tenor sax never needed a microphone. It packed plenty of punch. We would change uniforms at half time and had a movement routine with some of our songs. All very professional.

Rob Bradshaw, our lead guitar and his wife Carole have remained my valued friends and I have stayed with them in their Coromandel Whitianga home with its splendid views of the bay. They have returned to New Plymouth where Rob still plays in a group.

Sadly our pianist and friend Graham Pickett has died. Jim Fitzsimons, the sixteen year-old founder of the band and drummer is heavily involved in rugby in Hawkes Bay.

We played the current hits like The Twist and Rock Around The Clock till twelve at night and then, for a while, Latin, which really turned everyone on, with its wonderful rhythms. We would always start with our signature six tune bracket, including Harbour Lights, Moonlight Bay and Perfidia. La Paloma has recently had a two hour film made of it, being the most popular worldwide song, apparently. I saw the film recently and all the different country variations were exciting. We had a super young Maori vocalist, Robin Ruakere. He could sing well in four octaves and had to be a world star if he had been taken to the USA. He was so popular we did not dare put him on till half way through the evening as there would have been a riot if he had been taken off before the end. He became a doctor and was sadly killed in a road accident in his fifties.

I nearly suffered the same fate when returning home from playing in the band after midnight. I fell asleep at the wheel and woke for some reason, some ten yards from where I would have ploughed into the concrete side of a bridge. I deserved to have died. What woke me?

I became close friends with some of the farmers. Sadly, Don Blackbourn, a particularly nice fellow was killed in a bull dozer accident when a tree he was felling swung back and dropped on him. His super wife, Joan, was still alive in 2010 and sings Country in New Plymouth. Their daughter, Helen, when she heard I was returning to New Zealand in my late sixties, gave me a warm welcome, in spite of my losing most of my hair. Still got my teeth! She was only twelve when I was playing with the Daltones and easily impressed.

She married Lester Robinson a genius, who had his own electrical business aged nineteen and was sorting out various countries' problems before he was much older. A trouble shooter par excellence! He learnt early that you do not have to be brilliant in every field; just very good at finding the best people to work for you. I had a pleasant breakfast on their ocean going yacht at Manly not so long ago. Sadly, he died comparatively young.

Herd testing consisted of taking the full and very heavy buckets from the cows when milked, weighing the milk and taking a sample each evening. The process was repeated with the morning's milking and in the morning each test tube was put in a centrifuge spinner, having been mixed with concentrated sulphuric acid. This would separate the butter fat, which could then be read off. There, I just bet you were waiting to hear that! If you spilt a tiny dribble of the acid where your apron did not protect you, it would cut through the trousers like a knife through butter and you had to get into a trough of water p.d.q, before it reached your skin. I can still remember it happening once.

Playing in the band and herd testing did not take all day and night, so I also worked on farms sometimes. I dug a long drain through marsh for one farmer, wearing just swimming togs and wellies to keep the eels from biting my toes. An instant cure for athlete's foot? Sometimes I helped with fencing.

I walked back with one farmer and his cattle one afternoon as he was driving a cow back to treat her for bloat. This is caused by the cows eating legumes such as clover, which raises gas inside the cow and kills them if not treated quickly. We had to stop to treat another animal and in those two minutes, the first one was dead. Bloat was the scourge of the dairy farms at that time and he lost over twenty cows in one year. Treatment was either to drench them, make them swallow from a bottle, a fatty mixture that caused them to belch or more drastically, to drive a hollow pointed tube into their stomachs and then remove the plug to let out the gas. Now you know what to do if one of your guests has wind! Massey Agriculture College near Palmerston

North, which I attended for a few weeks, had a cow with a glass window in her stomach about nine inches long by four high so they could observe the results of different diets and the bloat cures. Quite amazing.

One dear girl had a crush on the tenor sax player, and told me that if we got married, her dad would eventually leave us his farm. She was pretty but the thought of being wedded to the wrong end of a herd of cows did not appeal. So that was that.

The Daltones in full swing

30

Young Farmers

WHILE IN TARANAKI I was chairman – not person – or even Chair, of the Young Farmers Club. We went on a trip to the South Island in mid-winter and stayed on various farms. I helped feed the cattle one morning when there was a beautiful white frost on all the bushes and trees.

They called for a volunteer in the local Otago rugby match. Otago just happens to be one of the leading clubs in New Zealand. Without thinking, I volunteered. I should have learnt discretion in the army. I did a superb flying tackle on someone, who swerved, leaving me to bounce on the ground right in front of the grandstand. What an idiot I felt! In the last minute I was passed the ball. I ran unopposed to the line and just as I was about to score, one ex All Black tackled the top half of my body from the right and another the bottom half from the left. When I picked myself up from the ground, after everyone had left for the changing rooms, I had a black eye and concussion. I staggered through the showers and was whisked away to a party.

The first party I survived but during the second, I found a Mackenzie's desire to fill me up with whisky did not go well with concussion. I was almost out on my feet. They wisely took several of us home in the open back of a pick-up truck and the frost soon sobered us up. I spent the night on a mattress on the veranda separated from the frost by a sheet of plastic.

We visited the oyster factory at Bluff on the Southern tip of South Island. We were allowed to put our hands out between the flying oysters and the tins they were destined for, to taste the specimens. Delicious.

Having completed my Herd Testing experience, I took a job for some months on the Hawera Demonstration Farm. I had to cut and weigh specimens of grass from various plots every day. We had pigs to feed and cows to milk and I had to record the daily temperature, rainfall and humidity. One day I made a mistake, possibly after a late night with the Daltones, and the local paper next day printed: 'Hawera swelters, while New Plymouth freezes.' They were just sixty miles apart!

Our kind manager paid me well to travel sixty miles to the Daltones' gigs and then back again. He even asked me to spend a few days up in Hamilton on tour with the band, all expenses paid but I could not spend so long away from work.

I visited Lake Taupo, an enormous caldera lake, where the top had blown off a volcano, millions of years ago. It was possible to catch a fish on the edge of the lake and swing it round into a hot pool to cook and then eat it off the hook. The area has boiling water not far below the surfaces. The Maoris use it for central heating in some villages. When cruising along the lake someone lost their hat overboard. I dived in to grab it before it sank and discovered the launch was already hundreds of yards away. The hat's owner must have had very slow reflexes. We were right out in the middle of the lake so I was saved a long swim when the launch eventually returned.

Ruapehu and Ngauruhoe are two volcanoes, which are active from time to time. Ruapehu covers the area with ash just to remind people that it is there. It has a major eruption about once every fifty years, the last being in 1995/6. These eruptions evacuate all the water in the crater lake and have created havoc as over a million tons of rock and mud gush into the nearest river. People ski in winter so it has its uses.

31

One Hill Too Far

ONE DAY I was invited to a party in Hawkes Bay, about two hundred miles plus to drive. I had a great time dancing and meeting up with old mates from Homewood. The Belle of the Ball was undoubtedly Fiona Williams, sister of Pete from the Homewood group. She was radiant and gorgeous but spoken for. Still one can look and admire.

I decided to leave about twelve at night and drove my thirsty Vanguard up and up into the mountain range. I had plenty of petrol when I started but the fuel needle steadily fell till I reached just short of the top about one thirty. There was a property with its own petrol pump. I stopped close to it thinking: 'Wonderful!' We still used three syllable words in those days – 'I will spend the night in the car and buy some petrol in the morning.' It was the coldest and most uncomfortable night of my life, beating the chicken shed by ten degrees. At six thirty I had had enough and staggered out of the car to stamp my feet and swing my arms. A farm worker appeared and my spirits soared.

'Good day,' I said. 'I've run out of gas. Might I buy some to get home?'

'No,' he replied. 'We're not allowed to sell it. It's for our own use only.'

Stunned, I thought for a moment. 'What the Hell am I to do?' The place was called 'Erehwon' or 'Nowhere' backwards and fittingly so. It was many miles from anywhere, let alone a petrol station. 'Okay,' I said. 'Just tell your boss. I'll stop here till I die.'

At this he turned on his heel and disappeared into the house. A few minutes later he reappeared. 'The boss says I can sell you enough to get to town.' Which is how I got out of that sticky situation.

32

Fresh Pastures

AFTER TWO YEARS of herd testing and playing with the Daltones, I decided I was not getting anywhere in life and would spend a few months back in Wairarapa before returning to the UK. I had met up with Ian Maclean, a young farmer from New South Wales, Australia and we decided to make a quick buck fence contracting. We were paid good money but took on a tough task as most of it was hillside fencing, which means dragging up the heavy posts to the site. Also the ground is rocky and very dry, so digging a post hole with a spade and crowbar was tough work. So we ended up very fit, bronzed and richer.

I worked for Geoff Bale, a decorated bomber pilot from World War Two for some months. He struggled to make a living and his wife, Pru, was often absent. I was in his cattle yards one day and unthinking, got off my horse. Now those cattle had never seen a human off his horse, having been raised in the Bush. They probably thought, when I detached myself from the saddle, that I was a dangerous alien that ought to be exterminated. So a cow charged me.

The yards were not made of conventional timber but faced with old airfield metal sheets, so there was no way I could climb out. The heavy mud underfoot also hampered movements, apart from the cow's. Inspiration made me charge the cow, raising my arms and bellowing at the top of my lungs and she put on all anchors coming face to face with me in astonishment. While she was wondering: 'What creature is this?' I evacuated the yard through the gate and was soundly told off by Geoff, who threatened me with the sack if it should ever be repeated. There was little fear of that!

A more pleasant event was duck shooting. We joined up with Don Cameron and a friend at first light and waited expectantly by the dam. Contrary to British custom, where it was thought unsporting to shoot them on the water, well warmed by whisky, Don fired at the duck on the water in direct line with me. Luckily the lead pellets just missed me but peppered the dam in front. I can't remember many duck being shot but whisky shares should have risen.

Geoff Bale was brother- in- law to Michael Moore. He won his DFC for when his bomber was shot down over Germany, getting his entire crew back to the Allies through German lines. A great man and good company, he was killed in a car smash while still middle aged. We got on like a house on fire and I miss him greatly.

After leaving Geoff as the work came to an end, I worked for Michael Moore painting the whole house and with two coats, achieved ten thousand square feet of paint. I count that one of my prettier assignments. It all had to be rubbed down with sandpaper first. Imagine that! During the evening till one thirty for many nights, I drove his tractor, working up a field for a crop. It was very cold at night and I wrapped my body with newspapers. Tramps know a thing or two and I sometimes sign myself: 'Super-tramp'.

To make some extra money to pay for my passage home I worked for a few weeks in an abattoir, cutting out kidneys from dead sheep. It was bloodless and so not so bad. I had been warned about some "bad hats" in such places and so when a Maori approached me in a threatening way, I drew my knife and was left well alone for the duration. The pay was very good and I had survived.

I went to stay with a Homewood cadet, Chris Sherratt, whose family owned a very large and historic spread in Hawkes Bay, Wallingford. He lent me a horse with a will of its own, so I pointed it up a steep hill and let it go. We flew up the first stretch but by the time we reached the top, it was mine! Chris asked me to go hunting with them but I opted out having never jumped fences especially topped with barbed wire.

I read a book and swam in their pool till they returned. Very kindly they arranged for me to stay a night with their cousins, the Geesons in Wellington, before I sailed for England. I was shown round the ship the next day by the Commodore of the New Zealand Shipping Company, Michael Moore's father–in-law, Captain Warren. On the trip, I was assigned to the Lieutenant's table and felt like minor royalty. The night before I left, I heard a band playing in a club and just happened to be carrying my saxophone, as one does. I approached the band leader and spent a very happy evening playing there.

33

Return To England And Penury

ON THE RETURN trip we might have been on a cruise. We stopped at Panama and some of the party went off to see a donkey perform horrendous acts, while others and I had a quiet time with rum and coke. I recognized the signs and hired a taxi back to the ship. I remember clambering up the gang-way and over the threshold and then woke up in my own bed next morning. The Devil looks after his own, as some cab drivers were said to rob their inebriated passengers and leave their bodies in a creek.

Our twenty four hours in Kingston, Jamaica were interesting. The market place was colourful with pretty native women dressed in outland-ish but effective swirling dresses. Before leaving the ship we were warned to keep to the smarter side of town as muggings of ships' passengers occurred every day. So I set off on my own looking for a swimming pool to cool off in. It was a pleasant area and I had no worries. A teen-ager approached me and asked if he could help as I looked a bit lost. I explained I was looking for a pool.

He said: 'Sure thing, massa. Ah can show you da way.' So I followed him for some minutes when another teen-ager joined us. I asked if it was far to the pool? 'No massa.'Bout five minutes.'

Another teen-ager joined us on his bike plus a fourth. I was beginning to get a little worried, with good reason. In a flash I was backed up against a wall and a knife slit through my watch strap in one fast swipe as he caught it in his other hand. Another slit my back pocket, which had the princely sum of ten shillings in it. As fate will have it, the watch had lost its winder that morning.

At this my temper snapped. I seized the lad's bike and swung it like a shil-lelagh round my head, roaring at the top of my voice. They fled and soon after a police car arrived, obviously called by a house inhabitant. Sergeant Savage, (what a wonderful name): 'If you'd killed da bastards, it wouldn't 've mattered. We'da slung 'em in da creek.' I had to return to the ship holding the remains of my shorts in place.

We stopped at Tahiti with its gorgeous women, who presented us all with shell necklaces on arrival and then led us to a very intimate dance. No wonder the painter Gauguin spent his last years there. What a way to die!

We also visited Florida, where I spent some time in the Everglades telling little crocodiles that if they did not escape soon, they would become handbags. For half an hour in an amusement arcade I tried to get rid of five dollars on the one arm bandits. An American Colonel asked me home to his place for a meal but the ship was leaving too soon, much as I appreciated his hospitality.

We steamed up to Caracas in Venezuela probably to refuel with cheap oil but did not leave the ship. It looked a heavy industrial site and unappealing. Then it was Bermuda, which had no cars on their roads but many horse driven cabs, so very peaceful and pleasant.

34

Fog and Snow

WE ARRIVED IN England on December 3rd 1962. It was the second coldest winter in one hundred years. We docked in Southampton to be met by a dense and cold fog. It was a contrast to painting a house, stripped to the waist all day, browning in the sun.

Through my school friend, Henry Hitch I was lucky to find a job with his cousins, the owners of a herd of prize polled Hereford bulls, some of which I was to look after. They were the latest craze and one went to America for three thousand pounds, the current price at that time of a three bedroom bungalow.

It snowed heavily one day when I was due at work. The main road was clogged by a stream of stationary traffic so I went round the cars asking who had shovels or spades. Twelve had them including myself, so we set to clearing the road and opened it after about an hour of hard work. I got to work where I stayed for three weeks due to the road becoming well and truly blocked.

One young bull thought he would take me on, refusing to be walked along the lane. They had rings through their noses to which was tied a rope. He obviously had a very tough nose. So I turned him at right angles to the road and then let him pull back. He backed into a ditch filled with stinging nettles and brambles. He rapidly vacated the ditch and was remarkably docile after that.

I went to live in Bristol, with a school friend of my mother's, the Falconers. Damaris was a teacher and kindly taught me for another "O" level, to improve my job prospects, which I subsequently passed. Try as I might, I could not find a job and my savings were disappearing fast.

Eventually Roddy Rutherford paid me for my car I had lent him but that money also evaporated. I did earn a little laying some crazy paving for someone and some more for wall papering a room. Have you ever tried wall papering a ceiling on your own? Don't! I was at my wits end for as soon as I had half the roll up and had to move the step ladder, down it all came again. Somehow I managed but never again!

I had moved out from my friends into digs and owed two weeks' rent, had nothing in the fridge and three pence in my pocket. Because I had been out of the country, Social Security used it as an excuse not to pay me a penny of welfare benefit. They said I could come back in six weeks and try again. One can get very hungry in six weeks, even very dead.

With the three pence I bought a local paper and searched the job adverts. There was one to help for a weekend with Caseys, the large frame tent and camping shop. I was to help erect many frame tents for a public exhibition in the park and then look after them with two other guys, smaller than me.

That evening we were sitting on camping stools outside the deserted tents when a gang of about twenty yobbos arrived. There was a thirty yard avenue between the rows of tents and they strode along it, shoulder to shoulder, obviously looking for trouble. I told the other two to do as I did and I picked up an all purposes camping tool, a cross between a small shovel and an axe. As the yobs approached, we walked towards them, feeling rather like Custer's last stand. I picked the biggest yob and had every intention of finishing him off, if it was the last thing I would do on this earth. Remarkably, as if sniffing out my intention, their ranks split when we were about three yards from them, like Moses and the Red Sea, and they went on their way without a word. We had seen the last of them.

Next day I was offered and took a permanent job working in the shop. Money! What a wonderful thing to have. After a few months at Caseys, including one frantic time when tents were coming back by the dozen from holiday makers in Spain, bent into crazy shapes by terrible storms, I was having a quiet drink in a pub when I met Peter Clay, the Art master at Clifton College Prep School. He was also a housemaster. After our initial banter, he said: 'You can't teach can you? We have half the staff down with 'flu."

I said, 'Sorry, mate. I'm an ex sheep farmer. All I know is about killing sheep. I have never met small boys since I left school myself.'

Peter said: 'You'll do. Nothing to it.' So that is how I got into teaching, a great career, by the remotest twist of fate.

I met the Headmaster and was duly taken on as a temporary teacher. Asked to do Latin, I opted for Geography and entered my first lesson like this: 'Morning boys, this is a skinning knife.' And you know, I never had any discipline problems. Can't understand why. Not then, nor fifty years later.

As his staff returned from their sick beds, the Headmaster thanked me for my work and said: 'You know, you're a natural. I will try to find you a job with a friend of mine, if you are interested?' That suited me fine and shortly after, I was engaged on the staff of Stubbington House Prep School,

Ascot. After these enjoyable three weeks at this prestigious school, I was superfluous again and had to fill in a couple of months before I could start at Stubbington.

With my recent earnings I decided to go skiing in Switzerland – where else? There it was wonderful. Plenty of snow and space. The first day at Saas Fee, with no idea of how to stop, I went up a lift to the top of 'The Gun Barrel', so named because going down that narrow slope, you had to come out like a bullet. Well, I stayed on my skis till emerging from the Barrel and bounced on my backside for at least seventy yards before coming to rest beside a very deep ravine. Another of my lives gone, the first being in Amman and another at the bridge I had nearly hit in New Zealand.

In the next few days I did learn to stop and even how to stay upright over rough territory. It was the greatest sport of my life. In a later trip I was travelling 'off piste' or cross country and skiing down a narrow track, bordered by trees and banks of snow covered earth. The track got increasingly icy and I was hard put to stop using parallel skis so had to snow plough, which was fairly ineffective. Eventually I was forced to plunge into a mound of earth, except it wasn't. As I hit the rock at about fifteen miles an hour, both skis snapped but luckily, not my legs. Live dangerously!

During the Après Ski, or evening activities, I fell in love with a beautiful German girl, a Countess. Judging by her ermine stole and her general manner, she was from the top drawer but in a different league from me financially. We got on very well, but I could sense it was leading nowhere. I was right.

I shared a room with an older experienced skier from Czechoslovakia, Evalt Osers. He was an interesting fellow having been in Intelligence during the war at Bletchley, working on breaking German codes and to do with Enigma. He lived in Shropshire with his wife and when I lived up there after qualifying as a teacher, we used to play hectic games of squash. His squash was fine but he introduced me to one of his colleagues, an Egyptian who had excellent skills including, if faced with an impossible return shot, placing the ball in the middle of my back! Two can play that game!

35

Stubbington House

STUBBINGTON HOUSE WAS the Prep School, boys seven to thirteen, where Scott of the Ant-Arctic had been educated and seven British Admirals. It had moved from Farnham to Ascot recently.

It was run by partners, John Renton and Arthur Moore and this was their first year in command. John was awarded the MC when with the Grenadier Guards he had part of his lung shot away. In spite of this he was still capable of supporting an entire small boy scrum leaning against him. A wonderful character and sadly deceased in 2010. He was learning Spanish in his nineties. Educated at Eton, he had a quick wit and sense of humour.

Some years later, when I was teaching in Sussex, he drove down to lunch with us in his Ferrari Sports car and I asked him how he had reached us so fast.

'Michael,' he said. 'No police cars can match this at 140 miles per hour.' They can nowadays so don't risk it. He also had a lotus sports car, the first with the receding headlights.

John's wife, Ruth helped in running the school of about one hundred and twenty, mostly boarders. She kept various Pekinese dogs, some hens and other fluffy animals, chinchillas, slightly incongruous for a smart Prep school but she had the panache to get away with it. Her family had a plastics factory, which might have helped John buy a new, exotic car every year.

I joined the staff with two other musketeers or virile young men, Andrew Walters, who was the son of a Shropshire vicar and to become a most popular and successful headmaster of Litchfield Cathedral School and John Bardolph, till shortly before that time, a player of the famous Harlequins rugby team. None of us were qualified except for our enthusiasm and natural ability and none of us had taught before. Yet our guinea pig clients did pretty well academically and on the sports field.

Years later I visited Andrews's school and stayed a couple of nights there when his delightful wife Sally was alive. A ten year-old boy asked me if I would like to hear some music on the grand piano. He first regaled me with some beautiful classical music and then launched into Scott Joplin's Entertainer, played fast and very well.

The choir boys all had to play several instruments and were a delight to listen to in the cathedral in Evensong. What talent! I was very sad to hear Andrew passed away recently. He will be missed by many.

At the end of the day we would use the local pub as our watering hole. John and I have often got through a large steak and then affronted the land-lord, a crusty fellow, by asking for a second meal, together with a bottle of red wine with each. After one such session John offered me a lift back down the half mile to school on the pillion seat of his Scott motor bike. We were up to one hundred and forty four miles an hour in a matter of seconds. 'Not so tight. You're throttling me,' he gasps. 'I'm falling off the bloody thing,' I reply.

John was utterly at a loss with money and still is but lives life to the full. He now plays piano in hotels round Folkestone as he follows my advice at last. He can play anything from Jazz to Beethoven and I can accompany him on sax or trumpet with most. Mad as a hatter, he drove a box like Austin with no insurance, no licence, no M.O.T (Ministry of Transport Test certificate) possibly no lights, and parked it illegally on the pavement in South Ascot as we went to the local bug house to see a film. Of course he was fined for his sins. Great fun to be with; may he live to one hundred!

I learnt the hard way of the Headmasters' mafia when I took a cricket team over to a local school. We batted first and by tea time were still in and making a healthy score. Their Headmaster came over and said: 'Ah Faunce-Brown, you know it is the done thing to retire at tea time and let the other side have a go.' Well like a sucker, not ready to cause an international incident with a Headmaster, I gave way and cheated our leading batsman, Nicholas Graham, of winning a bat from John Renton for an unbeaten fifty. Then near five thirty, when the game was due to finish, the same Head came up to me and said: 'How about making it till six o'clock and giving your bowlers a chance to get us all out.' Well, I let them do so and just pass our score at five fifty nine. That is to my shame and I have never let anyone talk me out of a match since.

We had a temperamental music teacher and Andrew Walters was a prank-ster. On her birthday, he presented her with a nice iced cake but when she came to cut it up, it was just a tin iced over. Unfortunately the real cake was too slow in emerging and she ran off in tears, so the practical joke backfired.

A link with Eton College was my mother's cousin Jane, who had married Tom Brocklebank, now a housemaster at Eton. I stayed with them for a few days as a small boy and again on my return from New Zealand. I dined with the Eton boys seated at the end of the table and had on my left Winston Churchill's grandson, also Winston. . He went on to become a member of parliament like his grandfather. He died in 2010 from prostate cancer.

Tom Brocklebank was an Everest climber in 1933, the time before they used oxygen and other modern aids. They got quite close to the summit but it was before Hilary and Tensing finally conquered the world's highest mountain. His granddaughter, Serena, inspired by his efforts, climbed Everest, reaching the summit. Tom was also stroke for Cambridge in their three winning years over Oxford in the famous boat races. Some man! Tom had a strong sense of humour and in a reference he gave me, he said, "Michael plays a pleasing sax and is a great heaver of rocks," as I had helped in his landscaping.

36

A Lake District Trip

THE BOYS AT Stubbington were a joy to teach, full of fun and energy. The three just men took a dozen of them on a trip in the Easter holidays to the Lake District in Cumbria and apart from John's ancient car breaking down, all went well. We started with the Langdale valley and arrived at dusk after a two hundred and eighty mile journey. We pitched our tents and somewhere during the night those with air lilos started to rise and fall with the tide. I was not so lucky and got soaked. We had camped in a 'dry' stream bed! Next day was blowing a blustering gale and by the end of breakfast everything dried out, hung on a fence. We cooked over gas cookers and had porridge, bacon and eggs to fortify us for the climb.

Half way up Pike of Blisco I told the party to go on and meet me at the top, while I helped a man in a panic as his ten year old son was frozen in two senses in a chimney, a cut in the rock, which should have only been attempted by accomplished climbers. I had no rope and had to help the boy up the freezing face, knocking holes in the snow with my hands. When we arrived safely at the top, I told the man a few home truths and re-joined our party.

The Lake District seems to attract idiots. On another day I had to help down from that same mountain a woman in high heels. Yes fair dinkum! (For real)

The local publican, John, was a serious mountain beagler and would hunt hare all over hill and dale. So he was pretty tough though fairly short. One day a large town lout started to throw his weight around in John's pub, the Dungeon Ghyll. John asked someone to hold the door open and then lifted up the lout by the neck and belt and threw him out of the pub. He did not return.

Twelve to thirteen year old boys will follow you anywhere and have amazing stamina. We climbed three peaks one day, including the second highest in England, Helvelyn. On Helvelyn there is a plaque near the top where a man died and his faithful dog stayed with his body for weeks.

On a later trip we climbed Helvelyn and arrived at Striding Edge. It is a razor back path, so narrow that you can inch your way along with one leg on one side and the other leg on the other side. It was covered in ice that day and not realistic for other people's kids. However we had left part of the group down below and they would be needing some action very soon. So I told the other teachers to take their party back the way we had come, while I went the quick way back along Striding Edge.

Not far along there is a little plaque to some poor soul, who had slid the thousand feet down to the bottom. It filled me with joy! The other side you only have a six hundred feet slide down to Red Tarn – named after the blood shed? Well the lower group were pleased to see me but not half as much as I was for the reunion.

That same trip, John, who had been at school at Sedburgh, a fairly tough college, told us he would like to take us across the tops to a pub, the Cross Keys, where he had arranged a meal for us all. We set out in slightly sleety conditions. All went well till we had been struggling against the wind blowing in our faces for an hour and it started snowing heavily. I was already questioning John's sanity, as he persisted in wearing only shorts on his bottom half and was turning a nice shade of purple. After another twenty minutes of very unpleasant conditions, with fifty yards visibility, I asked John how much further as the boys were getting worn out and we did not feel much better. I was seriously worried that we might lose some. He replied that it was only another forty minutes or so.

'Right!' I said. 'If you want to go on, you go on alone. We are going back.' So we all turned back and with the wind behind us, blowing at least fifty miles an hour and the sleet less painful, we plodded along what seemed for ever. I had a boy under each arm and in the last stages, was propping them up. We staggered down the mountain and sought refuge in a pub with a roaring fire. We ordered hot drinks all round and the publican provided blankets for the boys to wear while their sodden clothes dried out before the fire. It was a lesson learnt and we were very lucky it was not one of those tragedies one reads of in the papers.

We safely returned our charges to their parents at the end of the trip and started our shortened holidays, while I mentally resolved to always take a rope on future trips and to assess proposed routes more carefully. Also, not to put too much faith in the 'experts'.

During the breaks, the virile young men took cricket nets while a much older teacher, who was an MCC member, read the Times over coffee. It was only years later that we discovered the older teacher was just five years older than me. He always found time to go to county matches at the Oval but spent little time coaching the boys, who might have benefited greatly from his 'professional' expertise.

One hears today an awful lot about how discipline has failed ever since they banned corporal punishment in schools. If only they taught teachers to keep the kids busy, to talk to their pupils less and listen more, to use their sense of humour and to let the kids know that they really cared about making them all a success in some field, much of the Discipline problem would go away. Instilling two way respect would also help. Having said that, if parents just let their children evolve, without learning right from wrong, and do not show any love for their off-spring and don't back up teachers, they will only discover too late that little monsters grow into bigger monsters. 'This paragraph might be written into the motto of every training college,' says he modestly.

37

Hooked

ON SOME EVENINGS Andrew, John and myself used to meet at the five star hotel, the Berystede where I asked the receptionist, Daphne Hender from Launceston, Cornwall to cash my cheque. She had lost her dad in Holland during the war. His brother had the other share in the Launceston tannery and made a fortune during the war making boots for the services. She was quite clever backing the Ascot horses and we had several meals 'on the bookies'. We melded pretty well and before I knew it, I had proposed to her. She accepted and we were married during the summer holidays, 1965.

We honey-mooned on my meagre savings and the first night we stayed at a plush hotel at Banbury. The hotels gradually lessened in grandeur and by the end of the week we were in bed and breakfasts. We went up to Scotland where it never rains. Only pours! We visited the Duke of Argyle's beautiful home and admired all the armour and weapons on his walls. A wonderful collection of shields, swords, dirks and spears offered themselves. There are the expected family portraits back through the ages and heavy furniture, some with the attractive designs of the French, Scotland's historic allies against the hated English.

We were climbing the lower reaches of some obscure mountain when a grouse rocketed from under Daphne, somewhat disturbing her equilibrium. On our return I tried to visit the loo in Edinburgh, at the most twelve paces from the car and was drenched to the skin. We left Scotland just in time as a river burst its banks as we were passing and a torrent followed us much of the way to England.

38

Bulmershe Training College

AT THE END of an enjoyable year teaching basic French and middle school Maths at Stubbington, I went to Bulmershe Teachers' Training College in Reading, Berkshire. It was 1964. Although a mature student, I spent the first year living in the hostel with much younger companions. One night a party was in full swing still, approaching one o'clock. I needed some sleep and decided that enough was enough. I opened the door and stood saying nothing for a moment, clad in my pyjamas. Silence descended.

'Right, Ladies and Gentlemen. All good things must come to an end. Time for bed.' I would not have been surprised at catcalls and being told to get lost. Incredibly the party ended then and there. They all cheerfully eased out to their beds. Whether single or shared is another question but peace was restored. And next morning it was as if nothing had happened.

Being a mature student, I was eligible for a concentrated two year course rather than three. At the end of the summer term Daphne and I found a flat in Russell Street, Reading. They were all terrace houses. Fifty yards further up the street on the other side we heard there was a brothel. No, not tempted. The inhabitants of the other side heard strange noises in their lofts from time to time. On investigation they found that a Pakistani family had bought the house at the end and many were living in the lofts of the other houses right up the street, there being no fire walls. The inhabitants of the houses probably attributed any noises overhead to rats.

In the downstairs flat lived a young couple, who enjoyed having ferocious quarrels. They must have enjoyed them. Otherwise they would not have had them, would they? Tired of the incessant fracas I lowered my tape recorder down the stair-well and recorded a particularly nasty quarrel. When they had ceased, I played back the tape at full volume. They could not complain, could they? It was their noise. Anyhow they stopped arguing in our hearing.

For a wedding present John Bardolph kindly gave me a 1928 Jaguar, complete with walnut facia and huge headlights, plus as an Australian farmer once said: 'running boards wide enough for sick sheep.' It needed quite a lot of attention including changing its front to side panels, which I replaced free of charge with brand new ones from the Exchange and Mart magazine advert, where someone simply wanted more space in his shed. I blew apart much of the front with a blowtorch and by the time it was reassembled, it looked a treat. It wound up to eighty five miles per hour pretty fast but took longer to stop.

Daphne and I went away on holiday and I foolishly lent the Jaguar to a student, who professed to know all about old cars. When we returned all my time and energy had been wasted. The idiot had never checked the oil, which was fine when we left and the engine was ruined. I tried putting in new pistons shells but the crank shaft was ruined too. I had neither time nor energy to work on it as the next term began and the car eventually ended up in a scrap-yard. It would have been worth a fortune today and I have not seen the like on a road for the last twenty years.

Daphne worked for the Electricity Board in connection with way-leaves, where routes of power lines were mapped out. We should have stayed there another year and then I would have got a degree, but when asked by Principal Hollis if I would stay on and perhaps change from being Treasurer of the Students Union to becoming the Chairman, I stupidly declined. To have obtained a degree at this stage would have vastly increased my chances of early promotion and saved years of studying part-time while working at the same time. Hindsight!

39

Apley Park

I WAS APPOINTED as a teacher of Maths and English to Apley Park State Boarding School near Bridgenorth in Shropshire. This stately home was set in magnificent grounds near the looping waters of the River Severn. The headmaster was Mr Schultz, of advanced years. Most of the boys had dads in the armed services abroad and were there for a stable education. One eleven year-old, Brown, a good name, walked thirty three miles on our sponsored walk and raised over one hundred and twenty pounds for charity, a supreme effort. By way of comparison, my weekly wage then was thirteen pounds a week.

We were let, rent free, a cottage in the grounds, a semi next to the deputy head's. It was the same vintage as the main house with attractive stone, built to last five hundred years or more. When we first asked the Williams round to coffee we all sat on boxes. Eventually we bought furniture and haunted second hand and antique shops. I bought a nest of three antique tables for four pounds, ten, valued now at several hundred pounds and a lovely wooden chest of drawers. Also an upright steel framed piano for twelve shillings and six pence, delivery free. It probably still resides in the cottage, too heavy to move.

I learnt to canoe in the river water warmed by the discharge of the local power station. It was close to the famous Iron Bridge built by Brunel and also just down the river from the pottery firm at Coalbrookdale.

The Head decided to stamp out smoking, which was rampant among the boarders. Quite right too but I cared not for his method. He made the offenders sit in a room, its windows and door shut, and smoke countless cigarettes, with a member of staff supervising. Nowadays it would have been against their human rights. I opened the windows while I was in charge, and let us all breathe.

The day would start with a half mile run along the drive, followed by a swim in the indoor pool. The housemaster had them all swim in the nude, which I felt peculiar. Attitudes had changed since 1952.

One of the staff was an explorer, John Paisley. He hospitably had me round for a drink and we got through a whole bottle of whisky. I felt pretty crook next day but had my revenge when he came round to my cottage and I was in charge of the bottle. He had super photos of the South Pole, where he had spent many months.

The headmaster of the local comprehensive school, Richard Neal, came round to play squash in the Apley Park court with me. Later we watched a rugby match. He liked my rapport with the boys and soon after invited me to join his staff as a Year Master, responsible for the Pastoral side of one hundred and sixty nine boys and girls. Also to teach English. So at the end of the year I left Apley Park for The Phoenix, Telford, much to Mr Schultz' disgust.

Recently I made contact with some of the ex-Apley Old Boys.

One has a local pub, another drives huge trucks in the USA. A third runs a restaurant.

40

Phoenix

PHOENIX COMPREHENSIVE SCHOOL was comparatively small – about 650 boys and girls aged 11 to 16. Its catchment area was an old mining area with fairly high unemployment. Its pupils were as pleasant as you might find anywhere. Great kids, which just goes to show that being poor does not have to lead to Crime or Brutality.

Richard Neal was the only true genius I have ever met. He had survived the war as a fighter pilot, and that takes some doing. He pulled up the school from being the worst in the area to being level pegging with the grammar schools that take all the cream of the catchment area.

After my rugby team beat the local Grammar School team eighty six to nil, their headmaster would not speak to ours. Richard Neal was an outstanding teacher as well as headmaster. He seemed to know all of Shakespeare's works by heart. He could paint brilliantly, play from Beethoven to Scott Joplin on the piano very well, make up a witty poem in his bath before an evening dinner, build numerous boats for his children and shine at anything he set his heart on. When he retired, the same school reverted to being At Risk very quickly. What a waste! It just shows that you need first rate Heads and the rest will follow.

I was teaching one form of thirty nine top stream lovely pupils and switched them on too well. One twelve year old produced a story she had written over the weekend for homework of twenty neat pages. Correcting was a task indeed. I also took among others, a fifth stream class and was meant to introduce them to Shakespeare. They were fifteen years old and semi-literate, so I started with sex and somehow diverted to Julius Caesar. All those bodies! It worked. We were away. With Shakespeare, I mean!

I started After School Activities, first with a shooting club using air rifles and then was offered a full size, good condition snooker table, so I approached an army parent, Lt. Colonel Bouverie Brine for a Nissen hut to put it in and asked the Council for a free low loader. We erected the Nissen hut one week-end, quite a feat in itself, and planted the snooker table in it. Midlands TV filmed us all day for about forty five seconds real-time. What better way to keep the kids off the streets than giving them activities after school, which may lead to hobbies in their old age or even to careers? The Public Schools do this as a matter of course. "Public" meaning Private in the UK.

We had a member of staff, who was well endowed with ample flesh. One day she complained of a stomach ache and went home early. Imagine her astonishment when out popped a baby! She had not been aware of being pregnant.

It was a time of union in-fighting and many of the staff appeared to be doing their best to sabotage the Head's enthusiastic improvement of the school. One teacher seemed to lead the dissent, and while only four of us out of forty were working all hours for the good of the children, this lay-about would be laughing at us in the staff room as he worked to rule.

I was asked to wander round the school occasionally to make sure all was running smoothly and would find a certain mature teacher with his arm round a sixth form girl or reading the paper when meant to be teaching. It was virtually impossible to get rid of idle teachers short of rape in those days.

Daphne made our day by giving birth to our first son, Timothy in 1967. Unfortunately he was subject to illness caused by twisted gut, and he would scream poor child, for much of the night. Shortage of sleep, when working so hard, made things difficult. However it was a joy having for a while wondered if one of us was sterile.

We were renting the old school house at Oakengates and had our lead waste pipe stolen twice, so reverted to plastic. I revisited the place only a few years ago and found it still standing but boarded up. Rather a waste of a perfectly good house. The rest of the building next door used to rock a couple of evenings a week with the local youth club. We had a beautiful black cat, which we gave to one of the boys when we left. I am sure it was a very good home. How are you doing, Robert? That was the boy, not the cat!

In May 1969, our daughter Caroline was born. She was no trouble as a baby or later and developed a quiet sense of humour. At school she did everything asked of her pretty well and developed into a useful cross country runner.

41

Windlesham House Prep School

AFTER TWO YEARS of successful teaching and rugby matches, the Union in fighting became too much for me, and in spite of heavy pressure from Richard Neal to stay, I took a job as Head of History and Geography plus one of the House Masters at Windlesham House, Sussex. One of the older Prep Schools in the country, it was the first to introduce girl boarders to accompany the boys. It had been run by the Malden family since it began in 1837. It had high academic standards and I helped the Head, Charles Malden, even giving up my Sundays, to coach rugby. We had two unbeaten seasons with the first fifteen.

Charles Malden, Headmaster of Windlesham House,, was ex S.A.S. and looked like a film star and Elizabeth-Anne his wife, also looked as if she could walk into Hollywood any time. They both had First Class Honours degrees. They ran the school most efficiently, with weekly tests on Saturdays to show the children's progress in four subjects one week and another four the next. There were frequent reports for the parents, too. The atmosphere was very relaxed and it was and still is a leading school with many high powered parents and ex pupils. Discipline and academic rewards were through the old stars and stripes system and corporal punishment was unheard of. Classes had a maximum size of twenty. When I joined, the first six girl boarders had just arrived. The number of girls rapidly increased till they were about one third of the school population.

The main school building is a fine Queen Anne manor house. I believe the chapel that was added came from an Oxford College but might be wrong. There has since been added a huge multipurpose hall, big enough to accommodate the three hundred pupils they now have. It can be quickly converted from an auditorium with stage to an open arena for dancing or gymnastics.

My first self- imposed task was to paint my huge and rather grand classroom. I noticed that when it became an entertaining and reception room after I left four years later, they kept the colour scheme and it still looked fresh. It was full of all sorts of dyes, chemicals, a mongoose fighting a snake, assegai spears and was more of a museum than a classroom. So re-decorating it was quite a challenge.

At weekends some children went home. Those that could not, stayed at school and a duty member of staff laid on activities for them. I would arrange for two sides to play a sort of hide and seek in the woods and also took swimming in the indoor pool, playing my Boosey and Hawkes ex-army silver trumpet, while walking around to make sure there were no dead bodies in the water. It has a beautiful tone that not even I could destroy.

We had a brilliant music teacher, Ray Lorraine-White. He had played with ENSA, the group that entertained the troops in the war, and was wonderful on the organ. He had taught in South Africa. He told me of the strong pro German feeling with many of the Boers during the war. He had a wonderful rapport with the children, who were his substitutes as he had none of his own. He arranged the music for Oliver one year and I played the drums for several shows. When it was all over, I admitted that I had never played the drums before. "You can fool half the world half the time..."

On one show we nearly had a catastrophe as a major part of the scenery started to collapse. A twelve year old actor, Robin Briggs, nonchalantly leant against the scenery as he completed his words with cool presence of mind and won a roaring reception from the audience. He became a policeman, not a builder.

There was a gifted Art master, Ian Markland, who seemed very anti-establishment to be teaching in such a privileged school. I took advantage of the levels he raised the children to and my History/Geography room was festooned with my 'washing lines,' from which hung A3 pieces of paper depicting battle scenes, countries and their animals etc.. When over at Marlborough, which many of the children next attended, the Master (Head) button-holed me and said kind things about my rather novel way of teaching. The projects certainly worked. Average Common Entrance marks – that is the external exam they have to take for their next school – went up by twenty per cent. Also, revision was hardly necessary. The children would wander round in their free time looking at other people's creations.

The children were again very pleasant, as they had been in the Comprehensive school. Parents were supportive and we worked our guts out to make their children successful and happy. One new girl wrote back to her parents after a few weeks at Windlesham saying: 'It's like a holiday camp.' In fact they worked and played hard.

One of our pupils, Duncan Goodhew, went on to win an Olympic Gold Medal for swimming the 100 m race in Moscow in 1980 and was awarded the MBE for his services to Sport in 1981. He had lost his hair in a tree climbing accident while at Windlesham. He was dyslexic but soldiered on gamely with his studies. A very pleasant boy.

At weekends we housemasters would have groups of five or six children back to our homes for tea and television or games. I have a photo of some watching the landing on the moon in 1969. One boy is a doctor now. Not an astronaut. Apart from producing cakes for our young guests, Daphne made over seventy chocolate cakes one year for the school Sports Day. Quite delicious and what an achievement. It was interesting to see the twelve year-olds join our toddlers Tim and Caroline playing in our sand pit. Every garden ought to have a sand pit. Very relaxing and so cheap to make. Just remember to have it netted to keep cats from using it as their convenience!

I used to take shooting as an activity. We had a motley collection of .22 rifles. One was a lever loaded Remington. One had a pump action loading mechanism. It was imperative to teach gun lore or best practice before we began. One of those rifles would kill a sheep at half a mile distance, a local farmer friend informed us from past experience.

While at Windlesham I started my film making career with the children. The school had a super eight camera and I took a group to the local village, Washington with its pretty South Downs backdrop. We made a short documentary of the history and geography of the village, which I later showed at the Visual Effects exhibition at Olympia, where the school had a stall. Two County Chief Education Officers sat down and watched the film and were suitably impressed, which was gratifying.

The Downs being chalk there were no local streams so the farmers used the thousand years' old device, the dew pond. First you dig your pond. Then you lay a layer of clay, then a layer of flints, then a layer of straw, then more clay puddled down by people walking on it in bare feet. The result produces plenty of water from the morning dew. I wonder it has not been tried in Australia. If yours does not work, don't sue me. It's probably sprung a leak.

We held annual sponsored walks for charity and raised over a thousand pounds. It was pleasant walking over the South Downs. They were scattered with flint and it was amazing how corn could push its way up between the little rocks. Archaeologists reached the bottom of a Roman well they were excavating one day as I peered over the edge. It must have been a feat digging it in the first place. The local area is rich in History, including the famous Roman Palace, Fishbourne, with its beautiful mosaics.

Tragedy stalks all of society's strata and I was shattered to hear some years later that a very beautiful child, who must have become a stunning woman, died from drugs when hardly an adult. What a terrible waste. Such a delightful personality.

Daphne and I were host for some months to a young and gifted teacher, Richard Martin, who had yet to find accommodation and whose equally gifted wife, Rachel was to join our staff a term later. Richard is highly intelligent and great company, and we much enjoyed his presence.

Richard and I took a group up to the Lake District fell walking one holiday. We had a rather ancient mini bus and its gears would jam when it felt like a rest. One rainy day, when half the group had opted to stay in the dry at the warm church hall we had been kindly loaned by the vicar of Ambleside, we were playing snooker or cards and it was early evening when Richard's group should have returned. I was horrified to see two policemen appear. Thankfully they were there to inform us that Richard had rung them to say the bus had stranded his party but they were safe. All was well in the end but it was a worrying moment as accidents happen in the Lake District too frequently. I heard of a man killed when falling only fifteen feet.

One tough walk we experienced was a trudge around Fairstone Horseshoe, near Ambleside. There were six inches of snow apart from near the dry stone walls, where it had banked up to three feet or so. We set off on a fairly clear day but as we neared the summit a white-out set in. Visibility was down to about twenty yards. Luckily I had a rope and attached each boy to it, with myself leading and the other end attached to another teacher. There were twelve boys, a reasonable ratio. I had to stop and check my compass and map every couple of minutes. On one side there was a fairly steep drop onto ragged rocks and the other side was little better. The distance across the top, from one side to the other, was about fifty yards; not much to play with in those conditions. The snow was blowing in our faces and although all were warmly clad, checking the map was not much fun. By careful if ponderous wading forward, we reached the other end and descended out of the snow.

On another occasion we were traversing Green Gable, a smaller outcrop. We stopped to admire the view on this warm and pleasant day when I noticed a black cloud scudding towards us. 'Right lads, pack up fast.' We did so and had to contour walk, keeping the same height, till the wind hit us. 'Get down and cling on!' We had no rope as we had not anticipated trouble at the lower height. The wind was over one hundred miles an hour and I shepherded everyone into the lea of some small rocks until the worst had passed. The experience graphically demonstrated how quickly the weather can change in the English Lake District.

Richard and Rachel stayed at Windlesham all their teaching years and became its greatest supporters when one Head, after Charles Malden had died, let the school run down in alarming fashion. Again, what a difference a Head makes. Happily the school is thriving again and as ever, the best will survive through financial storms. I still saw them on their trips to Australia, a great thrill. They are without doubt very gifted teachers and have kept up with past pupils all over the world, giving them a wealth of people to visit on their travels.

42

St Peter's Prep School

WE LEFT WINDLESHAM for me to spend a year at St Peter's Prep School in Devon and then to take over as salaried Head after a year when the Head and present owner would retire. In the meantime we were to live in as House Master and Wife. Tim was nearly six and Caroline four. St Peter's only had about one hundred and twenty boys; forty of them were boarders.

The school had a number of Royal Marines' sons, on the whole a pleasant bunch like their parents. Daphne and I were invited to the Marines' Ball, a wonderful affair, with breakfast being served at three in the morning. There were two bands playing in tandem, and we had a splendid night's entertainment.

The staff were mostly unqualified and so, cheap. The Deputy Head, David Pearson, had been in Canada for part of his life. He was very pleasant but a little twitchy; I don't know why. One master, who had better remain nameless, would twist a boy's ear or bring down his desk lid on his knuckles. When I became head, he would be the first to go. The school building, a stately home and its pretty grounds were owned by Admiral Peters, a friend of my Aunt Alice. I taught the top English and some French. The day boys were a really nice group, mostly from Topsham, so local.

The matron had a room along from the boys, while we had a very nice bedroom and one for Tim and Caroline. Matron spent much time washing a senior boy's hair as he lay in the bath, which I did not like. She had a huge boyfriend, who came in at night, slightly the worse for drink. He did not actually cause any damage but it did not seem right, in a boarding school. I was in an invidious position as the Head would not have backed me. If I had become Head, it would have stopped immediately, so I had to turn a blind eye and bide my time.

One day I found a senior boy coming out of our sitting room downstairs. He made some weak excuse that he was looking for me. This happened again at a later date. I realized later that he had been going through my desk trying to find the letter from the Head to me, saying that I was to be a salaried Head. He had sprung upon me since our arrival, that he expected me to buy the school, having got me there on false pretences.

I approached the Prep School association the IAPS for advice as what to do. They said although they would support me, since the man had little money, there was no point is suing him. Our great friend, Claude Peter, a solicitor from Launceston said: 'Don't touch the school with a barge-pole.'

Since we had no money apart from that tied up in our little cottage in Wales, it would have been foolish to buy the place even though the Head had said I could have the school if I paid the bills owing, currently about eight thousand pounds, for nothing more. When I rejected that, there was an unpleasant undercurrent flowing till we left at the end of the school year.

The Head would go up to a boy waiting in the lunch queue and pull his hair for no reason, while smiling evilly at me. I felt like belting him one but that would have solved nothing. I resolved to stay on at the school till the new purchaser took over for the children's sake. Clearly the man was not at his best. He was said to have ill health. Maybe, but that was no excuse for brutality.

I have a picture of Daphne and me at St Peter's in our last term, when the atmosphere between the Head and us was electric and we look like total zombies, both worn out and at the end of our tether.

43

The Holy Family Middle School

THANKFULLY WE LEFT St Peter's at the end of 1974 and I found a job in a Catholic Middle School in Langley, Slough, just off one of Heathrow's runways, so every time a jet took off or landed, I would have to stop teaching, and that was every forty five seconds. There was no double glazing so the noise was intense. The children were from eight to twelve years old and I had a class of twenty two twelve year-olds, which is small in the State system. Ideal for teaching. I taught all subjects apart from Religion and Music. With Maths, English, French, History and Geography I have no problem but Science was very hard having never taken a Science exam in my life. However I taught a little about electric circuits without electrocuting anyone.

I also took soccer and had the pleasure of one of the best goalies in the country. Andrew Martin was approached by a couple of talent scouts for London Clubs when only twelve, for their juniors. He only let in three goals in the season, probably helped by the reserve goalie, acting as centre back so he instinctively was in the right position if ever Andrew was in trouble. We won our few matches and the boys enjoyed doing so. Andrew asked me whether he should become a professional footballer or aim for something else. In the circumstances it was a very difficult question. He was a bright pupil, alert, well-motivated, good looking and had everything going for him.

I said, 'Andrew, you would make a really good goalie but you could get injured early on and never play again. You will probably finish your football career at the age of thirty six or thereabouts. You will then have a similar decision to make. You have everything going for you academically and should be a success in anything you choose. In the end it is your choice. The best of luck.' I wish I knew which way he went and what happened to him. I am open to invitation to coach the English football team, but only if Andrew is our goalie!

In my first week at the school the priest asked me out to a club for a drink. It was in a darkly lit long building. We had a chat about the kids mostly. After an hour or so I noticed men working their way round the room with collection boxes. I asked the priest what they were for. He said: 'For the IRA'! I replied that I was not giving for that. He said: 'For Christ's sake, pretend to give something.' So I went through the motions for my sake!

I felt a complete heel when saying goodbye to the kids, who all lined up to give me presents after only one term. One child said sadly: 'Don't worry, Sir. No teacher has ever stayed for more than a term.' Heathrow and schools don't mix! They might like to think about that when considering another runway.

44

Leighton Middle School

I APPLIED FOR an excellent post at a new Middle School, nine to thirteen: Leighton Middle School. It was in Leighton Buzzard, Bedfordshire in the Midlands and in the spacious grounds and buildings of the old Grammar School. So we had a fantastic stage with dimmer and masses of hidden electric plugs, which I was to exploit fully.

The intake was mainly from middle class parents, fully supportive of the school and a charming lot. One parent came to me at a parents' meeting and introduced herself as Mrs Thomas. I proceeded to tell her what a splendid pupil he was, only to notice by her reactions that something was out of step. Eventually it transpired that it was the wrong Mrs Thomas! I didn't even teach her son!

The school was only taking in one year's pupils for the first, two for the second and so on, so we had our full complement of four years just before I left in 1979. A gradual build up into a first rate school.

In such an attractive location the excellent Head, Peter Jenkinson, was able to find top quality staff. The music teacher was terrific and she soon had a very tuneful and large orchestra. I was Head of English and also Resources. Two top jobs in one. I was given over twenty thousand pounds – a large sum in 1974 – with which to stock the library. It lacked for nothing and we had overhead projectors and a maps and poster cabinet and all bar the kitchen sink. I also had the nearly full time services of a real jewel, Mrs Jill Bridger as librarian. She was always cheerful and efficient and loving with the kids.

As ever a 'Do it Yourself' man, I needed a double electric plug in the Resource Centre, so opted to do it myself to save delay. I was trying to remove the protective cover with an insulated screwdriver when there was a blinding flash and the screwdriver end melted. It was some old and unusual powder insulated wiring and I was lucky to survive. Is that Life number four?

I took the Drama for the first two years till we had a full time Drama teacher. I put on a shortened version of Oliver and was thrilled when one little girl said to me behind the curtain, with shining eyes: 'They really like us!' It made it all so worthwhile. Our Art Teacher, Peter Clarke, would spend half the night painting every tile in the roof scenery and all the rest. The music, as said, was terrific. The show went with a bang.

There was the site of an old stately home near Leighton Buzzard. Peter Clarke found its rubbish tip and introduced us to bottle hunting. He had many shelves of ancient bottles in his digs. We, as a family, found some interesting bottles but they are long gone. I see in the Antiques Road Show that 18th Century bottles can be worth over one thousand pounds each. So much for litter!

My second production just for my class, Linden, a quarter of the school, was 'The Russians Have Landed' by some unknown author, Faunce-Brown. It only had six songs and some banner waving and Cossack dancing plus the story but went again with a bang, especially when our homemade tank – erected out of a supermarket's trolley – fired very realistically. Drama with responsive kids, (and aren't most of them?) is very rewarding. It gives them confidence as they find there is something they can shine in and helps with their speech skills.

I also took the soccer team my first year, before things got too hectic. I was given generous free periods in which to establish the Resources. We Dewey classified the thousands of books ourselves. Previously I was always involved in Rugby and a newcomer to soccer, but could not go wrong with a team that had an average Intelligence Quotient of 125. Whatever I told them, they did perfectly, no credit to me. We beat all the local schools and I tentatively arranged a match with a team in the next county. Their P.E. teacher told me: 'We have won all our matches but I expect it will be a good game.' I kept quiet and smiled to myself.

The match started with a couple of quick goals to us. One was curled from a corner into their goal. I have never seen an adult do that. Then I told the boys to walk it. They did. As one of the opposition was about to tackle, an immaculate pass would go to another of our team. They walked the ball right into the opposing goal. This totally demoralised the other team and we beat their invincible side ten to nil. What kids!

Eventually we went as far as Luton and had to wait on a freezing day out on the pitch for an hour till our opposition were ready. As they came out to play, smoke rolled across the pitch from a factory chimney on fire. I could not see halfway across the pitch. We lost that match by a single goal because the other side knew their way round their pitch better than us!

We had a frightening incident one Sports Day. The audience of parents and friends were seated at one end of the ground and the P.E. teacher must have lost his mind. He had the javelin event aiming towards the spectators. Obviously they were some distance away but the image still stays with me when a well-built Polish lad picked up his javelin and hurled it down the course. On and on it flew till at last burying itself in the turf about five yards from the nearest spectator. Phew!

While living in the Midlands we visited Silverstone race track and saw the most spectacular motor cycle crash one could hope for. The cyclist came off his bike at somewhere near one hundred and eighty miles an hour and executed the most perfect cartwheel of four rotations. Having landed on the grass, he lay there for a moment and then got up and walked away to our relief.

45

Our Welsh Cottage

WE HAD INVESTED in a Welsh cottage near Newcastle Emlyn, a pretty tree fringed part of Cardiganshire, with Cardigan, a pleasant market town, ten miles away. The cottage was semi-detached and conveniently our Welsh Nationalist neighbour's son could not burn out the hated English without setting fire to his own house. Having said that, his mother very sweetly brought over a delicious cake for us on our arrival and she was the best of neighbours.

Before I could apply for a Council Grant, I had to build a lay-by in concrete opposite the house, as it was a single lane road that ran past us. I removed the five feet high earth bank that ran about fifteen feet parallel with the road by shovelling the earth into a wheel barrow and emptying it in our orchard opposite. Having prepared the forty feet by ten feet for the concrete, I chose the hottest day of that summer to lay it. A huge mountain of concrete was disgorged out of the lorry, moving so as to spread it along the route as best it could.

Then it was over to me. Concrete starts to set as soon as it meets the hot sun, so it was a race against time if I were to avoid "Mount Concrete" instead of 'Cartref' becoming the name of our cottage. I dug feverishly, spreading concrete in all directions, pausing for the occasional drink of water. I had come over from Surrey two hundred and seventy five miles away for a four day break on my own. It was a question of raking it flatter before it set irretrievably. At last I had done it, and looked trembling at the lay-by already set hard, in places; a battle won only just.

The cottage only had one bedroom and a bathroom upstairs plus a funny little cupboard with a sky light and a low space also with a window for an airing cupboard. Downstairs there was a tiny dining room, a good sized living room with open fire and an equally small kitchen. Also a large coal shed on the same level. The bathroom moved to the space at the top of the stairs, and we had a builder put in a coal/wood closed in fire in the living room. I then knocked down the corrugated wood shed at the far end of the coal shed, which became a very nice sitting room.

I pulled down the chimney on the outside of the bathroom and dining area so its base could become a large cupboard. While at the top of the ladder, fully extended, a pot of paint in one hand and the brush in the other, I discovered a very active wasp nest. I continued painting very slowly and managed to complete the task without a sting. By the end of the summer holidays, we had a double bedroom upstairs still, a single where the bathroom had been and another downstairs and a very pleasant cottage it was.

There were masses of apples in the orchard and the plum trees round the lawn were laden so you could fill a bucket with a couple of sweeps of your arms down a branch.

We lived in our cottage for the whole summer holidays after I had left St Peters. As I painted the higher part of the walls outside, the ladder slipped and I was left clinging onto the roof with one hand and holding the large paint pot plus brush with the other. A good clip for the goon show! Daphne came out and could not stop laughing. Eventually I pulled myself up the roof and eventually reached the ground with no paint spilt.

We once went to the local church and were surprised to find in this country so famed for its singing, that there were no hymns. A very dull service and a sermon lacking in any humour.

I should add that the lady, who had sold us Cartref, was furious with me for not accepting her offer of four thousand pounds to buy it back. I had well-earned that profit with blood and sweat, if not tears.

With the money made by selling our Welsh cottage, bought for two thousand pounds and sold eighteen months later for eight thousand, we bought a nice house in Leighton Buzzard, Pond Cottage in the prestigious Heath Road. I added a closed porch onto the front getting a "brickie" to build on the foundation I laid. That made room inside for a dining area. I also laid the base and got a "brickie" in to do the rest on our strawberry patch at the rear of the house, making the poky little lounge into a spacious and comfortable room.

During our first autumn at Pond Cottage, we had two boys to stay for three nights from my previous school, Andrew Martin and Michael Wade. The priest drove them up to us and we showed them there is more to life than the concrete and noise of Langley, Slough. We took them to the local park with our children and they ran wild in so much greenery and freedom. Grass, apart from their litter strewn football pitch in Slough, was a novelty.

We also took them to Whipsnade Zoo, where lions and the rest have ample room to exercise in pens of an acre or more. There was a phenomenon at Whipsnade, an explosion of tiny frogs. Imagine a carpet of millions where one cannot place a foot without treading on several – extraordinary! We drove through the monkeys' enclosure without losing our windscreen wipers and refrained from feeding our spellbound guests to the tigers. The long weekend was a great success and more people should try it. When Michael's dad arrived to drive them home, their horizons had widened.

In both 1975 and 1976 there was a drought across all the south of England. Lorries were convoying from East Anglia to normally wet Cornwall with straw bales for cattle and sheep to eat; straw that is normally just for bedding or burnt off so the next crop can be planted. In Leighton Buzzard the pond shrank to a quarter of its size but I had discovered an underground cistern in our garden holding several hundred litres, with which I kept the garden alive.

The trick is to buy the worst house in a good area and do it up. I put in double glazing myself so you could see but not hear the traffic going by. I painted the house inside and out, and laid the foundations of the garage. Once again I had taken on more than I could chew with the concrete, which arrived late in the afternoon. The dimensions were eighteen feet by ten and six inches deep. Imagine levelling all that on your own as darkness is approaching. I was doing the final operation, smoothing the surface by pulling a large piece of timber back and forth across the floor. It was almost dark and snow had started to fall. I was virtually stuffed. Out of the semi darkness came a voice: 'You look as if you could use some help.'

A complete stranger knelt down and took one end of the timber. Together we made a good job of the slab. He got up and before I could ask him his name or where he lived, this angel faded into the darkness. Why is it only the bad we hear about?

In 1977 Christopher was born; so only two years old when we left for Surrey. After losing Nicholas at birth, it was a great relief to have our final child healthy with no problems, till he reached his mid- teens! Just joking!

As if life were not full enough, while I studied for an external degree with the Open University in my free time, I joined the L.B. rugby club and coached mini rugby on Sunday mornings. Henry Clarke and I, with much help from keen parents, took the club in two years from one to eight teams. When we went to play Buckinghamshire, we had quite a convoy. In those days, parents generally knew not to get out of control when watching matches although once I did stop a match I was refereeing to tell one dad it was only a game and to tone down his yells to his unfortunate son or I would stop the match.

46

More Qualifications

IN MY LAST year at Leighton Middle School, I was very lucky and got a sabbatical year to take an Advanced Diploma of Education to add to my Teacher's Certificate and O.U. Degree, which overlapped with the Adv. Dip. Ed. for six weeks. I lived in at Jesus College at Cambridge University and was supplied with bed and breakfast plus evening meal by the good warden. By chance, that had been my father's college back in 1920. On Friday evenings I drove back to Bedfordshire and my family. "Who is that strange man, Mummy?" Very strange!

Cambridge by Night

Yellow, murky neon drifting through the mist.
Beery laughs, bodies lurch, another cycle missed.
Youth clings close in chapel shadows; reverberating walls.
Grinning gargoyles spy their union by condescending Halls.
Half-hearted moon takes refuge from chilling fog,
No witness will it bare as drunken fool skittles
Students from his path in car too wide for streets
Narrowed by rows of workmen's lamps guttering in the damp
With unblinkered glance in forbidden territory.

I completed my course – Gifted Children, Maths, and various other aspects of Education – at The Homerton Cambridge Institute of Education several weeks early and watched some good cricket at Fenners, the university ground as well as playing an excellent player squash and exploring some of the pubs. It was all very relaxing after the pressure cooker that I had put myself through. I wonder what became of Michael Morrow, with whom I strolled the paths at lunch-time? Also Michael Hope, whose wife drew splendid sketches for one of my books?

In spite of my row of qualifications, I found no success in applying for deputy headships. There was a certain attraction in teaching in Middle Schools, since children of nine to thirteen are keen to learn and most pleasant to teach. So I soon found that for every job going at this level, there were seven hundred applicants. It was a disadvantage having been to a public school as the system was shot with envy and as Socialist as it comes. I decided to return to the private sector after a mad idea of buying a shop that mercifully fizzled out.

We sold Pond Cottage for twenty four thousand pounds having paid only ten thousand for it four years earlier. Not bad and it meant our next purchase would only have a nominal mortgage. Tip: Always opt for the type of mortgage that has you paying off some of the debt every year as well as paying the interest. Then with the aid of some inflation, the pain of the mortgage lessens by degrees, and you make a killing in the end.

47

The Hawthorns

THE NEXT SCHOOL was The Hawthorns near Bletchingley in Surrey. At that time, 1979, Reigate Grammar had started accessing boys of eleven and this hit The Hawthorns very hard. It was put about that boys would be more readily accepted by their peers at the age of eleven than at thirteen and gullible parents took note of this rubbish. So numbers were only at one hundred and nine when I joined the school.

The Chairman of the Governors, Anthony Stevens had forced the staff to take a pay cut or the school would go under. I refused to do the same as I was to be Head of English, History and Geography, with the huge responsibility of getting all leavers at thirteen to pass their Common Entrance exams to their Public Schools in all these subjects.

The Headmaster, Geoffrey Learner and his wife, Shirley had mostly boarders at that stage. They did a sterling job but life could not have been easy for them, with the school struggling for its existence. The roof had to be patched, rather than replaced. At one stage a petrol drum blocked the stream drain under the road and the ensuing flood almost reached the school cellars. We watched day by day as the water crept closer and closer to the main school building. Eventually the rain ceased and somehow the drain was unblocked.

Across the road from the school a businessman bought a large house and obtained permission from the council to have earth tipped on his land to make a sound barrier between the motorway and his property. He was charging the lorry owners to tip and having a large hill built at the same time. His only cost was a bulldozer and with lorries arriving frequently, day by day, the hill rose apace. He must have made a fortune. It just shows what can be done, using a little initiative.

Geoffrey and Shirley Learner are both musical and currently sing frequently in their retirement in Canterbury. Shirley was instrumental in training the school choir to a high standard.

The Hawthorns is housed in a 1624 mellow brick stately home, Pendell Court with a beautiful reception room and library areas. It is one of the leading Prep Schools in the country and has wonderful facilities in its over thirty acres of lush Surrey countryside. The present Head and his wife, Tim and Evelyn Johns have brought up its numbers so it has more children than some Public Schools. The ample sports fields and large covered swimming pool ensure physical activities are well catered for. But one should not forget that for every successful school there must be an efficient and dedicated staff, supportive parents and a strong governing body. The Web site is a treat and well worth visiting. Their Old Boys and Girls are also a strong supporting force.

The stained glass windows and beautiful carving were never endangered or hurt in any way during the many generations of children that have passed through that fine building. I firmly believe that experiencing beautiful surroundings has a valuable spin-off with the young, just like wonderful music. It makes youngsters appreciate fine things and respect them.

Anthony Stevens sold us a house with a third of an acre within three minutes' drive of the school for twenty thousand pounds. It was so cheap for Surrey even in those days because it should have been condemned. It had been built in eighteen sixty six as a labourer's cottage. The roof needed replacing, the front door likewise. All rooms had to have a metre of plaster stripped from their bottom three feet as rising damp was running down the walls. The gas pipe crumbled in our plumber's hand and so on. He said he would have had nightmares if he had known earlier.

Daphne was wonderful, putting up with living for months in a slum. She bathed our newest addition, Christopher in the sink and the whole family went to The Hawthorns for baths. I was quoted six thousand pounds for re-roofing so I did it myself for six hundred, including new battens and roofing felt. Many of the old battens crumbled in my hands and there was no felt. Most of the tiles were re-usable. While on the roof, some battens gave way and I was wedged upside down, crucified by a nail on each side of me, much to Daphne's amusement. Later, when the old roof was off a third of the house, we had a sudden storm and I was forced to scramble a giant tarpaulin over it. John Callow came to the rescue.

The garden was a jungle so the far end became a veggie patch and I laid out various flower beds. In doing so I found an old sink buried a few inches down and under that was a bumble bees' nest. They flew off to Bumble bee headquarters and left us in peace. A shame really. I liked their harmless presence. There were two large chicken houses, and using the best of their timbers, I built a good sized tool shed. Much garden rubbish had to be burnt at the end of the garden but under my bonfire lay a century's old cinders mound from the hearth. So when I lit the bonfire I was puzzled as it refused to go out.

After about a month of a smoking pile, I investigated and found a glowing volcano underneath, a metre or more across.

Apart from teaching, I used to help with the top rugby. We played carefully with the boys. The master in charge was a bully and he tackled me once, designed to show him as boss. I waited my chance and then gave him a "New Zealand" tackle. He never tackled me again. It was always hard to swallow, having led many teams to win all their matches, playing second fiddle to this not particularly brilliant fellow.

Later, when my eldest son Tim was at the school, I turned a corner and came upon this same man kicking Tim in a corridor. The bully offered to fight me. 'Yes', I said. 'But not in front of the children,' and I led the way into a vacant classroom. 'Would you like to start it?' I invited, feeling pretty steamed up, like he was going to end up the other side of that wall! Suddenly all the bluster evaporated. He started counting backwards from ten and muttered something about calming down. I thought perhaps I had better do the same or I might be had up for manslaughter. I told him he had better never strike a child again. Anyhow he never touched Tim again, nor did I see signs with the other children.

The French teacher was a World War 2 veteran, Lieutenant Colonel Denis Holmes. Lucas Phillips wrote "The Raiders Of Arakan" about Denis, He had been in the Ist Punjab regiment as a regular and was the British liaison officer in Burma. He would infiltrate the Japanese held territory, his fair hair dyed brown and also his body. He entered a village across a river, sheltering behind a sampan when nervous sentries scattered the river with machine gun bullets. He wore a loin cloth and strolled among the natives as one of them, after the invaders had put a high price on his head. He set up some ambushes as well as gathering information on their troop movements. Denis was an excellent teacher, although he could be a bit 'sparky' at times. He was an avid bridge player and Daphne and I had some enjoyable combats against him and his partner, Jane King-Smith.

The parents were most supportive and when I arranged for the school to pay for it, we built a pretty good assault course. There were monkey bars, a wall to climb, and various other obstacles. I planned it out with the boys in an eleven year-olds Maths lesson. Then the children and I went out and marked all the positions where the holes had to be dug, about thirty of them.

The next two Sundays Geoffrey Learner the Head, plus four parents, John Callow an Old Boy and myself dug the holes and erected the whole assault course. It went up like clockwork. 'This is how you dig a hole. ...Right, go and do likewise.' There is more to digging a hole than you might think. Perhaps I'll become a grave digger in my next job! Dig my own!

The children loved the assault course and some were incredibly agile and daring, swinging themselves over the net like true troopers or a circus act. Unfortunately, when I left the school for a while, other staff were not game to take it on and it rotted away through lack of use.

We had some parents of note including Kit Peters, who started Skirmish or Paintball, the game almost worldwide now, where one dresses up in protective camouflaged overalls plus goggles, and teams stalk each other usually in wooded areas. If your paint-ball firing gun hits the enemy, he/she "dies". We took the leavers on such a game one year and they thoroughly enjoyed it. Kit only had one leg and it was quite a sight watching him strapping back his artificial limb on the ski slopes. He was a brave skier and provided much interest on the slopes.

Another parent, whose name I had better not mention, was ex S.A.S. and rumour had it that he was the top advisor in a well- known hostage scene in Africa. His two sons were splendid boys and I hope they have gone on to shining careers, too.

Another Leavers present was to go up in a helicopter, which landed on the school grounds. I joined them being the master in charge of Leavers. Only six flew at a time, or was it three? We flew over much of the surrounding countryside and it was a noisy but enjoyable experience. One feels much more vulnerable than in a fixed wing plane. Just one engine and if that stops it is usually "goodbye world".

Yet another treat was a trip to the Royal Tournament. There was a bomb scare and we all had to evacuate Earls Court till the area had been searched. The Royal Horse Artillery do a wonderful ride as they cross each others' lines just missing by a metre or so at the gallop, pulling their shining field guns behind.

After school there were activities and all children were expected to join something, if only once a week. I have taken Drama and produced many plays, including 'Nero' a two hour musical I had written. I also took Shooting with .22 air rifles, indoor board games, including 'Tread Quietly' a Smugglers vs Coastguards game I invented, complete with matchstick firing cannon, which they preferred to Monopoly. I have never found the time to market it properly, but one day someone in the family might make a fortune.

Again, we had army type schemes where they had to learn how to move without being seen in the jungle at the end of the lake and also to cook over a camping gas stove, without burning the sausages, or their fingers.

48

Ski Trips

WE USED TO take school parties skiing in France and Italy during the Easter holidays. Parents came too and we took over two hotels. On the last trip that I was in charge of, a parent took my son Chris down a black run – the most difficult – when he had only been three days on skis. I was not amused... even when he bought me half a pint of whisky. Later I followed the man round a corner and found myself in the air where I remained for about twenty metres before landing upright to my relief and surprise. Later I landed headfirst in a snowdrift and cracked a tooth – such fun!

One day in the Italian Dolomites it was too cold to ski. I tested the slopes and found them a sheet of ice, with no hope of stopping or controlling ones destiny. So we opted to visit Venice. They say winter is the best time as the smells disappear. We travelled by gondola and passed magnificent buildings gradually sinking into the water, or perhaps it was rising. There was an atmosphere of past grandeur and decadence. All the main "streets" are canals and the magnificent buildings seemed uninhabited. There was no sign of life.

We visited the famous glass works in St Mark's Square and marvelled at the intricate patterns created by the glass blowers. Luckily it was in the dry season and we walked across the square dry-shod. The bridges belong to a fairy tale. It is a unique world and I was thankful for the ice covered slopes. St Mark's Cathedral or Basilica has a "Treasury" of magnificent paintings. It takes its name from the body of St Mark being stolen from its resting place in Alexandria in 828 and being brought to Venice. The Basilica was completed in the 1090's, even before my time.

On our return trip we passed cities built on the tops of mountains – quite enthralling. How people get up there, goodness knows. One supposes they were close to God, or perhaps retreating from the devils who lurked below. So we returned to the ski slopes and continued our suicide mission next day, after the ice had gone.

During this confessional, on another occasion, I slid upside down at least fifty yards down a very steep slope to the enjoyment of the gluevine drinking crowd peering down from a restaurant's balcony. There was sardonic applause.

There was a worrying time when a twelve year old boy had fallen off the ski lift and was lost. It was getting dark when at last I found him ploughing through snow above his waist, throwing his skis ahead of him, all of two metres, then digging down to find them, before repeating the process. It was hilarious but were we to get to the ski lift before it closed? If we failed, it would then involve finding our way down the steep mountain in the dark? Perish the thought! Thanks be that we caught the last gondola down. Just don't repeat that, James.

49

Clubs And Other Trips

I TOOK A film production club where the children made up quick stories with me and then acted them out in the house. We made a little detective story with bodies being discovered all over the place. Quite fun really. The editing package the school had was light years before Pinnacle and Adobe appeared but somehow we managed.

I also built a Stevenson Screen or a Weather Station and we would measure rainfall, temperature and humidity. Building it was quite a feat as there were one hundred and twenty pieces of wood, all of which had to have three coats of weather resistant paint. That again faded as no one else would take it on, when I became Head of Maths and English. Still painting was such fun!

We took trips to the West Country in the holidays, and on one with Simon Etchell, one of the pillars of the school, there was a colossal lightning storm at night, which we all watched from the safety of the hostel. Not long after this a state school on a similar expedition lost a child drowned when the teachers allowed him too close to a stream, which suddenly became a raging torrent. This marked the end to many school trips as teachers were afraid of legal proceedings. There was another terrible tragedy when several pupils were drowned while canoeing off the North Devon coast.

Another of our trips was to the Lake District in Cumbria. I have a photo of Christopher, our younger son, traversing a ropeway some twenty feet up, near the Dungeon Ghyll pub in the Langdales. They would also go pony trekking, orienteering, abseiling, rock climbing, canoeing, raft building and sailing. The assault course, which left them all plastered with mud, was a great favourite. The permanent staff cleaned them with a high pressure hose, which led to much laughter.

These outdoor pursuits were wonderful for all children but especially the plumper ones, many of whom had little self-confidence, being lesser mortals in competitive games. They learnt the value of teamwork and caring for others. They would come home bubbling with enthusiasm over their adventures and with a new self confidence that expanded to other avenues. To stop these pursuits for fear of litigation is so short sighted and deprives children's right to self-improvement. Those guilty of preventing such trips should be exported to Greenland!

In my later years I was Senior Master, which involved much pastoral time, and Head of Maths. We had an intake, which included a wide spectrum of ability. Blowing my own trumpet, in our external exam at twelve to thirteen years of age, the Common Entrance to Public Schools, we averaged, mean and mode, A grades for many years. The only parent I ever had a serious disagreement with, accused me of not teaching his son well enough and when he went on, as a very weak student, to get a B in C.E. Maths, he gave all the credit to an outside tutor, but as his wife had cancer like mine, I forgave him...just! Such pressure can lead to extreme behaviour, as I know only too well.

When Daphne had cancer she attended a Laying on of Hands event on several occasions at Loseley Manor, near Guildford. We became good friends with Sue and James More-Molyneux, such kind and delightful people. The Manor had become very run-down while James was away in World War Two, as a Major. On his return he found Sue desperate for pans to put under the many leaks in the roof. Ever resourceful, he started importing timber framed houses, which can be erected in three weeks, a profitable affair, and now the manor is well kept and they allow the public around on special days.

The manor had belonged to Sir Thomas More, their direct ancestor. The present house was built between 1562 and 1568 as the previous one was considered too small for Queen Elizabeth 1st to visit.

Sue and James had three delightful grandchildren, who served their guests at Christmas when we were among their guests. Tragically the eldest aged twelve was riding his little motorbike to help with the morning milking of their Jersey herd when his anorak was caught in the wheel spokes and he was strangled. The saddest event in this book. May fortune smile on the others.

50

Orme House School

IN 1984 I left The Hawthorns to become salaried Head at the all age school, Orme House, which had just been bought by a Lebanese man. He also had schools in France, Dubai and Beirut. The school had been run by two elderly ladies. A woman, who reminded me of the Gestapo, had been deputy head, and she showed that she resented my being there from the start. It was a relief when she left.

Most of the staff were unqualified but the Head of Maths and a middle school teacher were teacher trained and very good value. I had to get a living in teacher as housemaster as I refused that burden myself. Added to the usual pressures of coping with boarders, the owner insisted on my taking eighteen Lebanese boarders, one of whom was sixteen and three others arrived aged eighteen. The four older boys were clearly there to get out of being conscripted in the Lebanese war. The eldest three were no trouble but the sixteen year old lout Jim, personified trouble. I found him one day karate chopping into splinters new wardrobes just bought for their use. The owner had stressed that I should buy a cane and use it, but I refused. I have only ever used corporal punishment at school once in my teaching career, when a Lebanese fourteen year old boy belted a twelve year-old English girl very hard in the stomach. The staff were baying for his blood and I gave him one stroke on the backside with a gym-shoe. He did not repeat his crime.

Returning to Jim, I had to threaten him with my friend a local sergeant in the police force and some nights in a cell. The sergeant was a figment of my imagination but it worked. Later in the long summer holidays, Jim was on the phone from Lebanon pleading with me to let him return to school next term. I enjoyed saying: 'With your record! No way.' So I guess the army had the pleasure of his company.

We had a very supportive family, the Mylands, whose son, Dominic was very friendly with the Lebanese, and they frequently invited most of them out to their place for weekends. This took a lot of pressure off the house-master. One pupil from that part of the world was Talal, a delightful Saudi Arabian, who never put a foot wrong and was always cheerful.

The owner would tell the parents of his plans for turning nearby farm buildings into a super gym. There never were any signs that he really meant to. His aide, an attractive woman with no manners, would arrive in the school snooping around with no warning and never had the courtesy to come and see me first or to ask how things were going.

I managed to get some out of work Italian swimming pool builders to build a magnificent pool, with salt solution instead of the usual chemicals. When the school was closed a year after I had left, the owner had some construction work done and they damaged the pool, built for a song, beyond repair. What a waste.

Most of the windows were in a sorry state and very draughty so I had them all replaced with double glazing, leading to much warmer conditions.

As well as being Head and site manager, which were full time occupations, I taught the top English and although only one of my twelve students got an A grade in 'O' levels, it was the sole A in any subject. In fairness to us all, the school had more than its share of dyslexic and slow learners.

The school's owner refused to pay a tradesman's bill in full, just for the materials. He asked to use my office to talk with the very capable Irishman. I was amused to hear their heated voices and know you only take on the Irish at your peril!

I was working a hundred hour week most of the school year and striving my best to raise standards but the pressure was too great and I resigned, or to be exact, I went to hand in my resignation and quickly saw it would be to my advantage if the owner was to sack me. So we came to an arrangement, when I refused to join one of his other schools in Arabia, that my daughter, Caroline and son Christopher would stay on for a further year, free of charge. This saved me thousands of pounds. I had a letter of confidence from all the staff and parents just before this. The school was losing money simply because numbers fell dramatically when certain parents took exception to it becoming an "Arab" school and as eighteen of them arrived, eighteen indigenous folk left. I insisted all qualified staff were paid correct wages and in keeping with the owner's wishes and mine, engaged more qualified teachers. Orme House closed one year after my departure.

51

Building

ON LEAVING ORME House, I was immediately offered the post of office manager in a building firm, on a considerably increased salary with Project Pilots from Croydon, where I stayed for six months. It was useful experience as I was doing the job of a quantity surveyor there, which knowledge I used for advanced Maths projects for our scholars after they had taken their exams, as I returned immediately to The Hawthorns.

Twelve year-olds designed the new cricket pavilion, which was used as an alternative entertaining area. The architect made a plan and then changed it to almost exactly our offering.

I was asked by Martin, our boss, to be present at a meeting with a client who failed to pay our bills, and as a potential MI5 agent, I slipped a recorder into my pocket, switched it on, ready to record the evidence, in case of a later dismissal of the facts. All went well till the .... tape ended and it announced the fact with a loud bleeping. Martin gave me a hard look and I briskly got to my feet saying: 'Ah! That's the secretary paging me. Please excuse me.' as I stalked out.

As a minor Recession hit the building industry, half the Project Pilots team were 'let go', including me. So back to teaching.

About this time Daphne developed cancer. It soon invaded her in many places and it did not help when someone at the hospital omitted to flush her system after Chemo, so one arm became twice the size of normal. At a later date, I had to tell a nurse to flush her, or she would have had both arms swollen. This condition stayed with her till she died. However the Chemo therapy worked for a while and she went into remission for a year or two. Cancer hit her time and again through thirteen years, and put a strain on the family. She bravely fought it and soldiered on.

As soon as Anthony Stevens, Chairman of the Governors knew I was available, he asked me back to The Hawthorns to become Head of Maths and Senior Master, and there I stayed till my retirement in 1996. I produced many plays, including Nero again, The Government Inspector and Run For Your Life plus the romp, The Happiest Days of Your Life. It was hard work, on top of teaching full time and taking games, but good fun and the boys and girls enjoyed it. So did their parents, who went overboard with Nero.

During the '80's, our executive school governor, Anthony Stevens asked me to drive him up to London twice to the Fishmongers' annual dinners at the Guildhall, as he was in his eighties. They were grand occasions with a large glass of Champagne offered on arrival, to give one strength to mount the wide stairs, heralded by trumpeters on our way. I never realized I was Royalty! Well not since the days of Owain Glendower, the last of the Welsh Princes 1354-1416, who led the rising against Henry IV but was never captured. – A distant relative.

During the dinner, which lasted for about three hours, there were nine courses with a different wine lubricating each. At the end, just in case one felt dry, there was the "Loving Cup" a huge vessel and one took a sip before passing it on to the next member. While you drank, your friend would guard your back, as that was when you were most vulnerable. – History comes to life!

At one dinner I sat next to the Sergeant at Arms of London, a very high dignitary and we had an animated discussion about international rugby, our mutual passion. Opposite me sat Commander Noble, the chief organizer of the Mulberry harbours, so essential to the Allies' success during the Normandy invasion. They were floating concrete "quays", which were towed across the Channel and allowed our ships to disgorge our men and supplies in huge numbers very fast.

At another dinner, I was opposite two leading television producers. There were seven ambassadors present there and "little" me! A storm was flooding the streets when we left and since Anthony Stevens did not bother much about car maintenance, the wiper blades did not work on his tiny car. So I sobered up very fast, peering through the impossible windscreen.

I taught the son of the manager of The Dutch Swing College Band, the longest lasting band in Europe. It was started in the last part of World War two in a cellar in Holland , and was a bastion of resistance against Germany. One day Robert rang me up and said: "Michael, we have a free night. Would you like us to play at The Hawthorns?" Would we just! It was a marvellous night and they treated us the same as if we were a big gig in London. We had the twenty five minute drum solo while the rest of the band went off and "took five" and the Conger where the band walked round the audience playing hot jazz. What a night! Not an empty seat.

Robert Masters, the manager's son, distinguished himself on the last day of his final term by giving a bully a bloody nose. He said, "That's for giving me Hell all the time I've been here." Something I was totally unaware of. I said, "I never saw a thing. Well done Robert, if a bit late."

The Dutch Swing College Band

During the eighties I only visited London four times. Each time there was a bomb, courtesy of the I.R.A. When you walk into a street and are waved back from a cordon, it reminds you clearly of the perils in your own country, let alone those faced by all in Northern Ireland. And to think fund raising was going on in America to buy guns and bombs to kill civilians as well as British soldiers trying to maintain the peace! Our Allies?

During all those years of teaching, we could only afford one week a year holiday. We would drive down to Launceston in Cornwall, Daphne's home town, and stay with her life-long friend, Claude Peter, the senior solicitor of the town. He lived in a large house in a huge garden at the top of the hill. He was very generous and had given several acres to the local school for playing fields. He was a chain smoker and his study walls were dark brown with smoke from the ages. One can imagine what the inside of his lungs looked like.

Claude was due to have an operation on his throat when he died, which was perhaps a blessing. A wonderful friend.

We would explore rural Cornwall with its almost deserted beaches and our children searched for mermaids or whatever in the rock pools. They never found any. We visited one pub for lunch and although it was a cold day, as one gets in the Wet country in summer, the publican would not allow us to bring the children inside. So he lost our custom. Sometimes one wonders whether some pubs are open just for the landlords' benefit, and if they were ever children themselves. I was not amused!

The Lost Gardens of Heligan were a treasure we visited. Their Web Site says it all. The photos give a glimpse of their beauty. Situated in Cornwall near St Austell, they are a "must" for explorers of rural England. Owned by the Tremayne family since 1603, in William Shakespeare's life time, they fell into jungle after the first world war when all the male staff signed up with the Duke of Cornwall's Light infantry, only six out of twenty two surviving. The gardens were only "rescued" by Tim Smit, from 1990 onwards.

52

Retirement from Teaching 1996

IN THE FIRST year of my retirement, Daphne was written off by the local hospital and left in a room on her own to die with no one emptying the bins etc. I knew something was wrong when as I arrived, the Asian doctor assigned to her began shivering. I had her out of there in twelve hours and safe in the Marie Curie hospice in Caterham. After a few weeks in their tender care, she was well enough to come home and treatment was renewed, using a trial resource containing yew tree extracts, I believe the idea being to fight a poison with a poison. Anyhow she managed another year of cheating Death. We went on holiday and had a good time.

During Daphne's thirteen years of fighting cancer and the occasional remission, I learnt a few things: One, avoid stress. Hard if you have caught the disease, but Relaxation is the name of the game. Two, avoid red meat. Fish and Chicken are fine. Three, see as many comedies as you can. Doctors agree that laughter in some way releases beneficial chemicals.

If she had died from her first illness, Christopher would have been left without a mum, aged seven. As it was, terrible though an early death is, he had reached the age of twenty, and independence. I hope that in reading this, many will benefit from cheating the cause of thirty three per cent of all deaths in the Western world. One wonders why there is this sudden surge in cancer. Not entirely a coincidence that it started around the time of the Chernobyl disaster. Radioactivity was blown by prevailing winds all over the world.

Also, as the world increases in its 'Civilization' and pursuit of the money god, Stress grows fast. Many children I have taught hardly see their dads, who disappear from home soon after six a.m. and return after their bedtimes. Is it really worth never seeing their children so the mortgage can be paid? I am not subscribing to tents but many could survive with a less opulent home and life style. Some hardly see their mums as an au pair girl is engaged as nanny. Is it any wonder so many teen-agers are such a mess? I am a good one to talk. At school by eight fifteen and home at five thirty, only to bury myself in correcting and lesson preparation till ten thirty at night. Daphne said I was a different person after retiring. Oh dear! What does that say!

During the first year of retirement I had twenty five pupils I was coaching, mostly in Maths and English, and including four Plymouth Brethren whom I took in a group of four, three times a week also for Geography. The latter were sixteen as were two ex-Hawthorns boys. The Plymouth Brethren boys and girls were nice enough but they were inclined to chat amongst themselves, as no doubt they had done with my predecessor. I am not accustomed to ill-discipline and after some months, when I had prepared a really good lesson, they tried to continue their socializing, I told them what I thought of them, and there was a stunned silence as I walked out. Their organiser begged me to come back but I did not. I was pleased to hear they did well in their "O" levels. Plymouth Brethren are not allowed to go to theatres or cinemas or to watch television except in some cases a very carefully chosen programme. They cannot go to ordinary schools in case they are polluted and thus live their lives in an artificially remote manner, conditioned mentally to observe a protected and narrow form of life. They assist each other financially, which must help as adults and they run businesses efficiently.

Living in Australia, I see how Plumbers and Electricians are kings, going away on frequent holidays, paying for their children's private education and having a good life. It makes one question the idea that most children should go to university.

53

Property Makes Money

GROWING UP WITH parents, who are hard put to pay the next bill, makes one careful with money and to avoid making the same mistakes. Having moved back to my childhood's Devon, a year after Daphne died, I sold Oakley Bungalow for one hundred and eighty thousand pounds, having bought it for twenty thousand and spending about fifteen thousand on doing it up. So I was able to buy a pleasant but dull bungalow three minutes' walk from Dartmoor national park for one hundred and five thousand pounds and another new four bedroom house for one hundred and twenty thousand pounds, which I let.

I only mention this in case someone else is inspired to make money doing the same. Four years later, I sold the rented house making sixty thousand pounds profit and my bungalow for two hundred and twenty five thousand pounds. I painted the outside myself, making it much more cheerful, and as everywhere else, I put in secondary glazing, making it warmer in winter and cooler in summer. I put up new gutters all round and replaced most of the facia boards. Secondary glazing is where there is a gap of four inches, ideally, between the existing window and the new glass sliding windows. That is the optimum gap for noise reduction. Double glazing is sealed units where the existing window is replaced entirely; good for warmth but not so for noise prevention.

A huge oak tree at the top of the garden threatened to fall and crush my neighbour in a gale, so I had to pay for that to come down – in pieces. Son Chris teases me that everywhere I go I cut trees down. Well, I don't care for becoming a tree crushed purée.

I joined up the house with the metre distant garage, making the nearest room en suite with loo, basin and shower plus a roomy store cupboard. It rained for six months while I was doing this, except for a dry spell of three days. It is an unforgettable experience, digging an inspection hole for the drains, five feet deep and a metre square. Much of the time I had to split the rocks with a sledge hammer. I was usually plastered with clay. I employed a retired builder to build the floor, end walls and also a roofer. The builder had forgotten how to use right angles, if he had ever known and I spent ages straightening doorways and the window. – Aged sixty three. I guess I deserved that profit.

My last tenant, Mr John Goddard left the new house owing me two thousand pounds plus. He had been illegally running a second hand car business from it with a row of cars down the street. The police asked me where he had gone. I replied, 'Do tell me, if you find out!'

It took three mini bus loads to the dump to get rid of all their rubbish. The oven took three hours of hard scrubbing to get clean and they had left their broken furniture throughout. If anyone runs into a second hand car dealer called John Goddard in the West Country, remind him he still owes me two thousand, one hundred pounds plus interest, and if you can get it off him, send me only half and keep the rest for your efforts. Otherwise, just give me his address and I will do the rest!

Living in Devon, weather excepted, was very pleasant, in quiet Dousland, apart from a horrible little girl, who used to tantalize a resident dog by sitting just outside its boundary fence in the road making it bark. It was just far enough away to be bearable through my double glazing, but it never ceases to amaze me how adults will put up with that sort of behaviour, when surely they cannot enjoy incessant barking. Or perhaps they are all masochists, or deaf!

I walked many miles over Dartmoor and along the coast with a friend, David Hawking, who has a wonderfully funny way with words. If his poetry is ever published, buy a copy. It is very clever and a little naughty. We would aim for some Devon or Cornish pub for our lunch and sample the ale. Then for a Devonshire cream tea after the next leg. Yes, real clotted cream, unlike the synthetic substitutes sold worldwide.

The moor has its famous prison. Escapers risk falling into bogs or losing their way in thick fog. One such fellow saw a light to his relief in the distance. Soaked to the skin he staggered to the door of the solitary dwelling and knocked on it. Imagine his feelings as it opened and a warder helped him inside, saying: 'Welcome, me lad. We've been looking for you.'

My cousin Rosemary's husband John was Head of the local primary school and the prison chaplain. He says the children of the warders were a tough lot.

The Dartmoor church, a huge damp edifice, looms out of the mist like in a Dracula film. It was built by Napoleonic war French prisoners as their nearby gravestones testify. They were the first inmates of the prison, which was one stage more comfortable than the prison hulks at Portsmouth, their original "home". Its porous granite walls weep constantly.

On a fine day, Dartmoor is a wonderful place to walk, twenty six miles across with the odd pub, such as at Princetown, where one can find good food at a fair price and a blazing fire to warm ones fingers. It is well populated with sheep, which are not always looked after kindly in winter time and the famous ponies, which are rounded up annually so some can be sold, mostly for meat to the continent. Sir Francis Drake had leats or channels of crystal clear water built for the inhabitants of Plymouth. They are walled in by slabs of granite and still flow today. They help fill Burrator reservoir, set in its wooded beauty.

Goodbye Dartmoor

Once there was a moor of beauty;
Got its name from river Dart.
The grass was mown by sheep and pony.
Rock was moved by horse and cart.

Give us back our tumbling water
Crystal clear, our granite leat;
Sheep's Tor's steep and narrow pathways,
Or we'll hang you by your feet.

Common rights preserved for centuries;
Sheltered gullies and picnic coombs.
What's the use if we can't find 'em?
Fine old trees and ancient tombs.

The Water Board sent their bailiff
"Get your stock off our land!"
Gorse and bracken've taken over.
Stupid blighters don't understand.

No more sheep. They've all been slaughtered,
All the ponies for foreign meat.
Where's the guy who gave the orders?
Drown 'im in the nearest leat.

Threatened by those modern morons.
They couldn't plan beyond next week.
Now the moor's a "no-go" jungle.
No more walks or hide-and-seek.

At night I used to join Mr Sticks in pub gigs or at the Plymouth Country and Western events. His proper name was John Corderoy but he joined the Royal Marines aged fourteen as a drummer boy. He played Europe and that little place across the pond, the U.S.A. and went across to France once a year. If he had had a manager, he would have seen off the likes of Crosby and Sinatra, but he was happy to be just himself. We had some rare old gigs, on one occasion going through one hundred and eighty four songs, and played Devon and Cornwall. When we played in Plymouth and Sticks sang "Glory, Glory Alleluia" the hair would stand up on the back of my neck. – The only place I have any left! – It was truly a wonderful sound. Sadly he went into hospital for a leg operation and no one had told them to watch his blood count. He came out in a box, which I was very upset about.

I also played with Jim and three others including Billy Butlin Junior, grandson of the Holiday Park magnate. He was a champion drummer. Probably still is. And he would throw his twenty plus drum sticks stuck with glitter, up into the air, not missing a beat, and catch them again; only one or two at a time. He is a class act on his own.

We played frequently near Plymouth at a Country & Western club where they had shoot-out competitions. They only fired blanks of course and were timed on the speed of their draw from holster to aiming and firing. They were all dressed up in Confederate or Union uniforms, complete with curved cavalry sabres. An authentic atmosphere. We played as far North as Dartmouth and well into Cornwall. It was great fun apart from the smoke. You could see a thick blue blanket hanging in the air. When I went to the doctor for entrance into Australia, he told me that passive smoking had ruined two thirds of my lungs, revealed by x-ray. A bit of a shock. Curiously, apart from double pneumonia in New Zealand, my lungs feel fine now, possibly due to trumpet and sax playing. Also swimming five times a week may help. A check-up recently revealed that my lungs are A1. It just shows how the body can rebuild itself.

54

Film Producer

DURING MY FOUR years in Devon, I wrote a full feature film script: 'Fight Back' about an ex SAS man, who retires to a run-down Devon fishing port and is hassled by the local yobs. He defeats them by degrees and also the fishing bosses, who are exploiting their employees. The idea appealed enough to the famous Edward Woodward to want to be in the film, but I could not afford his fee. Still it was a terrific compliment to my script.

I decided to produce the film anyhow. I chose Ernest Goddard, who enjoyed my music in the Tavistock Arms on the border of Devon and Cornwall, as my lead actor. I was lucky enough to find the experienced Richard Fells as my sound man and having seen them in action the night before in a local drama school production, I cast thirteen actors next day in fifty five minutes. None of them let me down and Ernest was excellent. While on holiday with Chris in the south of Spain, I had overheard a man talking about his grandson at film school. To cut a long story short, Robert Waddilove became my Director and his mate, David Calub the cameraman. They did a sterling job; also on the editing, which was a huge learning curve for us all.

Robert and David stayed with me and the others commuted from their homes near Plymouth. I rented two houses from the Ministry of Defence. One we used for changing rooms and for refreshments, which were always available. The other became a den for the "yobs". Having toilets and kitchens was essential and very convenient. There were sixteen locations and only one cost me anything. A farmer supplied a herd of jersey cows, to block a road and two identical cars, one with no wheels or engine. There was also a slurry pit the yobs were to drive into, when the lane was blocked. Incredibly, his cars were the same model, and colour including sun roof as that of our leading actor. He even supplied the heavy machinery, which was going to knock down Ernest's houses.

I had to insure the production for ten million pounds. This cost me five hundred pounds, and I drove the stunt car myself to avoid a considerable increase of premium. It was an interesting experience as I had to miss the granite gate posts with four and a half inches on either side, while sliding the car. No dents!

The sun literally shone on us as well as metaphorically. There was no rain for the whole month we were filming. It started the day after we had finished. And this was Devon with eighty inches of rain a year. I found a sandwich lady from whom I had to collect every morning before the actors appeared. We had Dartmoor to film on during the day and at night. Any policeman coming upon us at one thirty in the morning, with our faces blacked, wearing balaclavas and throwing a body out of a moving lorry, might have had a fit. We did warn them.

A kind owner of a carpentry workshop let us film for three weekends in his very roomy building and would only accept a bottle of whisky and a show Video for his pains. We filmed at night on the docks on the moving pontoons, without anyone falling into the sea, having been told we could not film on the safe concrete part. This was really hairy. A Jazz café in Plymouth let us film on their premises.

The furthest we had to drive was about fifty miles away to the nearest canal, where Ernest was to find a body, only to discover it was a dummy I had borrowed from the Tavistock tip. This was where he 'rescued' a truculent teen-ager, Edward Scott, and took him home to give him motivation and a purpose in life. The men of the tip normally had their dummy and mascot dressed as a police woman and it was imperative that she was returned to them in immaculate order, having been dumped in the canal.

The icing on the cake was when the Plymouth Police lent us a police car plus driver for nothing. Really terrific of them. There was no fuss nor having to apply to Canberra for permission!

We used a JVC camcorder I had just won in the PC magazine plus my older JVC. For editing we used the first most basic Adobe, also won months later in the same magazine. Now I use Adobe Premiere Pro CS6. It is hard to learn but worth the effort. It will edit HD material also. Even 3D.

The DVD of 'Fight Back' was on the Net with Netflix for hire. They had bought it from Echelon Studios who had no right to sell it for resale. It was only on loan to them and they had no proprietorial rights. Echelon now have it in their catalogue, as witnessed by a member of my cast. They have no right to still market it and will be hearing from my lawyer shortly, if they continue to ignore me. When asked about this, Netflix have at last answered my emails. If one goes to court, only the lawyers make money, but it is a matter of principle. I thought of trying Blockbusters with a copy but to have it classified would cost over $700, which I would never get back. Eighty two minutes long, or twenty two minutes longer than Blair Witch, it cost me six thousand pounds to make. I only paid my lead actor and also the Director and Cameraman. Everyone else signed up to do it for free in addition to free food and drinks, a show DVD and the experience, which is of considerable value when applying for a job in the industry.

I did not hear a single word of complaint or argument during the very full month of shooting, in four six day weeks. Part was due to always having refreshments on hand, and proper changing and rehearsing rooms plus the toilets. The weather helped and all credit to Robert Waddilove, the Director. It was very tiring, especially for me and I would never take on another feature film without a line producer. Their job is overall organization regarding payment for everything that is needed and to get it at knock-down prices.

However it was great fun and a terrific experience. Remember if ever tempted to film, the world wants to help you. Just ask. In the UK at least.

55

An Historic Production

MY SECOND BIG film is a documentary titled 'Cross Roads In Time'. It is eighty five minutes long and consists of a series of interviews with people some of whom were alive even before the first World War. One was from Belgium and her family had escaped to Britain in an open boat, avoiding the minefields.

Another interview was with a farmer, who was a small boy at the outbreak of the second World War. He remembers the American soldiers staying on their property just before the D-Day landing in France. Earlier the Home Guard were suddenly assembled, including the man with a wooden leg. The small boy, shivering in his pyjamas, watched them march away up the hill, like the grand old Duke of York, to where they were to hold their positions with their ten rounds of ammunition and the odd hay fork, at all costs. False alarm! Luckily the Germans had not landed and they marched down the hill again for a nice cup of tea.

The same farmer saw a partially blind petrol pump attendant watching some idiot peering down his petrol tank to see how full his car was, with the aid of a lighter. Backing off, he said, 'Just wait a minute while I run up the hill and watch you coming down!'

I also filmed down the local copper mine, which had been the largest in Europe at one time. It is on the Devon/Cornwall border. My lights gave out and we had to depend upon our miners' helmet lamps. We were told of a cat that had disappeared down the mine and swum across a cave. It was eventually rescued, when its owner, an old lady, who lived in a cottage several hundred feet above the mine had insisted they search again after three weeks. She had this vision that it was still alive. The brave mining engineer swum across the cave when he saw two little eyes gleaming in his torch light. The cat scratched him though his overalls by way of thanks.

Another interviewee, a retired solicitor now sadly deceased, had a hard time down the coal mines, aged fourteen for he was over six feet tall working in tunnels four feet high. He narrowly missed being buried alive when the roof collapsed... luckily at night. The surveyors had missed a large fault line in the rock. The film should be of interest to Historians and others.

Talking about films, some of my favourites are: 'The Power Of One' that everyone should see, the story of a little English boy in South Africa, around 1942 having lost his parents. He was sent to a school of Boers, whose allegiance was firmly with the Germans. His treatment at their hands was quite frightful. Most moving and beautifully filmed. Then there is the wonderful escapism of the James Bond series with its humour and cliff hangers with poisonous spiders and snakes harassing the leading actors. Then for an ex boarding school inmate, the early Harry Potter films are such fun. That is what films should be: Fun, to escape monotony or sorrow.

56

Back To Teaching

As I WRITE this, I see on the Web an account of my teaching at The Hawthorns School, Bletchingley by the star of my musical, Nero. Modesty prevents me from repeating it, but many thanks, Nick Harrison. It is great to be so remembered by one. I shall never forget the scene where all the ghosts of Nero's victims return to haunt him. A coffin lies there, surrounded by mist and suddenly the lid opens and a head appears. The entire audience jumps. 'Got them!' I think. And Nick never missed a word or cue in three performances with a huge role to play. He is now a qualified architect with his wife and children. I wish them the best. Jackie Birch, our music teacher, did a wonderful job with the sixty singers.

In teaching one gives one's all and I thought, rightly or wrongly of all the children as my sons and daughters when I was younger, and then my grandchildren, when older. I tried very hard to be fair and to treat them not equally, as some have greater needs, some less, but as I would have liked to have been treated. When Headmaster Tim Johns said to me, 'They love you.' I was so embarrassed, I made some stupid reply.

When I started teaching Maths, I began to receive presents of chocolates, wine and the like at Christmas from my class of twelve to thirteen year-olds. When I said that much as I appreciated their kind gifts, I was not a great chocolate fan, the gifts grew till every child in the class gave me wine, vintage port or even Champagne. Well their parents did. Then it grew again – the same for the end of the summer term after exams. Then for the Easter term as well. I never had to buy alcohol for years. Their generosity knew no bounds.

When I retired from The Hawthorns, Daphne and I spent a very pleasant afternoon with Evelyn and Tim Johns. Two days later we were asked back to the school for I knew not what. I thought some misunderstanding had happened. Daphne must have been in the know.

As we drove up to the school, we were directed to the pavilion. When we arrived, a throng of parents and children present and past gushed out of the pavilion, some hundred and twenty plus. It must have been a case of: 'You breathe in and I'll breathe out,' as it was a large pavilion but not that big. I had to shake hands like royalty and was exceedingly touched. I was given a photo of myself playing the trumpet in a beautiful leather frame and a lovely pint tankard with its kind message engraved on it. Someone got on the piano and mysteriously my trumpet appeared, so a gig started up. A parent said I ought to have taken up music as a career and not Maths, which could be seen in two lights!

Then I was sent on a writers' course, all paid for, up to Inverness, Aberdeenshire in Scotland. I failed to see the monster but became one myself when I saw police pompously sending away youngsters playing the bagpipes very well to crowds of appreciative tourists. Is there no crime for them to attend to?

With the death of Mr Sticks, I wanted a new start and having spent my earlier four and a half years in New Zealand, I felt like trying my luck in those parts once more; countries with real summers and friendly people. I decided on a trip to Australia first.

57

1999 The Australian West Coast

I LANDED AT Perth and enjoyed this pretty little city on the wide river Swan. I was filming a sea plane which was taking off and landing in succession to check its noise levels for the council and got talking to the pilot's friend. He insisted I join him in a drive round Fremantle and then his wife gave me a splendid tea. He then showed me more, including the grave area where over one hundred Aborigines had been slaughtered. Then we had a huge dinner. They were wonderful hosts. I took them out for a meal but would love to repay their hospitality in Queensland or now the UK.

I visited Fremantle, that splendid old port where they were launching a replica of a sunken Dutch trader next morning. I enjoyed the music from a wedding group, who were ensconced in a café almost opposite a brothel.

That day I visited Rottnest Island and enjoyed filming fabulous little bays. It is well known for its diving potential. Its miniature wallabies or 'Quokkas' are quite cute and very friendly. A young boy said to his mates: 'Look at that man. He's talking to his camera!'

The same evening I shared a backpackers' room with five guys and a beautiful girl in her early twenties...Safety in numbers! The next morning I shoved through crowds to film the vessel being launched at first light. There is another island close by where they farm snakes for their venom. A venom milker? Not the job for me!

I drove with a touring company up the West coast of Australia from Perth to Monkey Mia in the north, visiting the Pinnacles en route. They are a wide area of wind eroded rock figures that assume the shapes of many different people from witches to monks. Let your imagination flow. We braked while a brown snake crossed the road and our driver caught a bluetongue lizard to show us. We stopped at Shark Bay and watched fifteen foot monsters lazily swimming by from the safety of the cliff top.

Australia boasts the world's three most poisonous snakes, The Taipan, the Black Snake and the Brown snake. If bitten by any of these, one has under four hours to get the antidote in a hospital, or one dies. I have only seen one Black, curled up by a walking track in the Bush, too dozy to harm one as it was cold, and unseen by the first dozen walkers passing by and the one

Brown, which Tim and I sprinted away from. Plus the two at the Wedge-tail winery, one of which tried to take on my car – and who says they are not aggressive! People lose fully grown cattle to snakes every year. Yet they are protected. Snakes are more valued than people in this strange land.

We bathed in a billabong and the others sang songs while I played the harmonica by the fire under the Milky Way. Matilda waltzed several times. Our driver Jim was also the chef. He was an excellent cook and we were fed like kings or queens, with plenty of vegetables and fruit carefully stowed in the cool boxes or 'eskies'.

The drive was boring at times as one hundred km stretch of desert looks much like another, but we stopped occasionally and took in the plant life sheltered by the scrub. At Monkey Mia, we watched the seals and pelicans being thrown scraps and went out in a boat, seeing a dujong or sea-cow, an immense floppy hunk of flab, the marine equivalent of our obese people. We also saw a large turtle swimming along, minding its own business.

On the return trip we went sand skiing. Climbing back up to the top of the dunes was very hard work, and having done much snow skiing, I was not enthused. Over all, the trip was fun and an interesting experience.

58

To Albany

AFTER RETURNING TO Perth, I spent a day or two in the Hay Street back packers, with a room of my own. The manager was a character, standing about six feet, six tall with broad shoulders. He said he had been Princess Margaret's body guard. It was hard to picture him squeezing himself into her car.

I joined the trip south. This was so very different. The countryside has more trees and very pretty bays, where it is safe to swim, even if the water is cooler. We saw some wind surfers on very rough water. They were a sight to behold, skimming the crests of the waves so expertly and appeared well above us on the shore. We swam in a beautiful lake and enjoyed a good old splash around, which I filmed.

Eventually we reached the giant trees, which are unbelievable. We saw the tallest fire observation post in Australia. There are three platforms up this tree, one at twenty five metres, the next at fifty and the last at seventy five metres or about two hundred and thirty feet. Most of the others climbed to the first platform. Having noticed that some of the iron rods up which they climbed were loose and seeing the few inches of safety wire netting on the outside, I decided to film their ascent from below and good luck to them. The gaps between the rods sticking out of the tree were at least thirty centimetres apart and they were only about forty five cm long from trunk to end. It looked highly dangerous. Thankfully they all returned to earth safely.

Then we climbed up the walkway, which looks down on the giant trees from above. This is well built and very safe. But what a feat to build!

We eventually reached Albany on the south west tip of Australia. There are rain forests galore with many brightly coloured fungi.

There is a narrow rocky arch from one outcrop of cliff to another. I believe it has since fallen. The trip was most enjoyable and I can highly recommend it. Incidentally, the climate around Albany is more temperate than in most of Australia. One caveat: A huge iceberg is said to be heading their way, and if it does not miss Western Australia, there might be quite a crunch!

After such a super trip I decided Australia was the place for me. In August 2002 I immigrated to Australia, on a Retirement visa. I flew from Heathrow to Melbourne, where I bought a Hyundai Sprint. This was a super car, and one had only to touch the accelerator to know it was appropriately named. There is a very good eating house near Elizabeth Street sharing the same stairs as MacDonalds. One can buy a meal for about eight dollars and go back for seconds or thirds, and with a huge choice of meals. The weather has always rained when I was in Melbourne. Someone must pull the flush cord daily. It was a fun town with youngsters painted in gold or blue standing around like statues, but don't pinch one as their reactions will be faster than you almost certainly. There was a superb juggler and someone on a bicycle trying to tie himself and his machine in knots; also an excellent steel band. I love their sound. Who manages to dent an oil drum into just the right shape for perfectly tuned notes?

On the way north I stopped in Canberra and busked in the main square. To be honest, I was not after the money but desperate for somewhere to practice my soprano sax. People started throwing money at me, well into my saxophone case and looked so hurt when I explained I was only practising, so I shut up and in twenty minutes had enough money to pay for a first class meal.

Canberra is a clean and pleasant little city, where one can see the country-side in both directions at once. I visited the excellent display of battlefields at the war museum and as always, was moved by the shocking waste of life displayed on the wall in endless names. The fountains were pleasant and I love a city in which I can find my way round. It has street signs and others showing the whereabouts of the theatre et al. A pity Brisbane cannot follow suit!

I drove through a bush fire at one stage. It had been lit by some idiot torching the car he had stolen, with not a care for the farmers who lost live-stock, feed and fences, and possibly their living, even lives. Arsonists deserve to be locked up in hot, airless cells for many years.

I slept in a motel somewhere near Tamworth and it sounded as if the endless chain of trucks was driving through the middle of my room. I picked up a hitch-hiker for company next day and all went well till he rolled himself a noxious smelling cigarette. I signed that he might follow the smoke out of the window if not very careful – remember the lungs – so he thrust half his body out of the window and continued his foul habit for a while.

People always warn one about the dangers of picking up hitch-hikers. Perhaps it is the latter who should be warned. I only pick up people of my own size or less and have carefully planned what to do if one should become dangerous or threatening. Take the car up to max speed. Point to something on the horizon on his side. Quietly release his seat belt and then do an emergency stop, waving him goodbye as he sails through the windscreen. No, I don't mean for picking his nose, but should it become a matter of his or my survival. 'I have an evil mind?' Possibly, but certainly a strong sense of survival.

At Coffs Harbour I spent two nights having asked the resident singer if I could join him for a couple of songs. Yes, we were still there next night. Music is a strong drug and having large and appreciative audiences fires one up.

Gympie was stoking up for the forthcoming musical shindig and already sporting a wide spread of mud. – 'Always a drought in Australia!' I listened to some indifferent buskers and bought myself a whip, which was fun to crack. It is best to ensure a fair distance from the nearest people.

The road north was littered with the corpses of kangaroos. Trucks all have huge bars across their engines to protect their drivers from live 'roos coming through their windscreens. They cannot afford to swerve or they'd end up in the ditch. At night, particularly around dawn and dusk the 'roos cross roads oblivious to or blinded by traffic. I only once drove in the dark before first light, intentionally to film them and was confronted by an emu, which considered it her road. Minutes later I had to stop as a large roo reckoned I was on his road.

Rockhampton was good value with its rodeo. I found hard to take the lack of applause for these excellent riders entertaining the crowd and risking life and limb – as shown by the ambulance carrying off a wounded lad at speed – Is it such hard work to show a little appreciation?

Townsville was as far north as I aimed to venture. It has a zero tolerance for barking dogs, which I considered very civilized. Dog owners, oblivious of the nuisance their pet pooches cause, personify selfishness in the extreme and should be left in a cell for a month with a recording on loop of their own dog in full voice, playing incessantly. They might get the point! Townsville is a pleasant clean town and I found an immaculate batch for the night, with showers available.

59

Travelling The Interior

ON THE NEXT leg of my journey I came across a genuine drover with a mob of about two hundred cattle. He was helped by a vociferous dog, and a lad on a small motorbike. It was good to see a glimpse of earlier years.

A pub near Emerald was entertaining. My expensive camera was too good to leave in my bedroom with no lock on the door. When I dared query whether there were any rooms with locks, the landlord glowered round the bar: 'There's no one here'll take anything of yours.' I believed him. The route to the far distant loo, essential once during the night, was along the veranda in full view of passers-by. There were no locks on the showers either, but they did not look as if they were over used.

I got talking to a hulk, a professional prospector. He had his own bull-dozer and appeared to be one of the larger operators in every sense. He was seeking a partner, but my rampant imagination pictured my two legs sticking out from under a mound of rocks, and I avoided volunteering. He reckoned to have spoilt over a million dollars' worth of emeralds with his large scale methods.

Gullible tourists are invited to pay a few dollars for the privilege of 'fossicking' through piles of debris to seek precious emeralds, no doubt well sieved by many others over the months. I joined them but never saw anyone leap in the air shouting: 'I've done it. Made my fortune!'

I arrived around noon in Mount Isa, a mining boom town and announced my arrival to a helpful music shop owner. I asked her if she would care to round up some musicians for a jam session that night. Incredibly before an hour had passed, she had five and we raised the roof that night, under the Milky Way – is that possible? They very kindly asked me to stay for a week but having nothing to do during the days would have bored me to tears so I declined. When I passed by to thank them next day, the pile of our beer cans was a metre high.

I then motored south to Alice Springs. It is no longer a collection of mud huts as in Nevil Shute's time but a fine town with fountains and much marble. The temperature ranges from 45 C. maximum in summer, down to freezing in winter and snow has been known four times in one hundred years. It has its own airport and a population of 27,400 people. It is equidistant between Adelaide and Darwin. On the downside the local "original owners" have serious drink problems.

Ayers Rock or Uluru was next port of call, 350 km south west of Alice Springs. As one approaches across the desert it stands out like an enormous whale. It is almost 1000 feet high and five miles round its base. It is a mystical place of reverence for the Aboriginal people. They would prefer tourists not to climb the rock but they still do, in spite of several falling to their deaths every so often. I saw the plaques in remembrance of some who had slipped and fallen, and decided not to climb. It is so smooth that once you slide from the ropeway, there is nothing to stop you sliding down the rest of the way.

I spent a pleasant evening playing with a band in a local township. If one has the cheek, it is easy to join up with groups, provided there is a free microphone and one fits in smoothly without stealing the limelight.

Next stop: Coober Pedy the opal centre of the world. As far as the eye can see, the barren landscape is riddled with holes, pits and tunnels dug by past prospectors. The general impression is similar to the surface of the moon, not that I've been there lately. Nowadays the tourists are not allowed out of their vehicles because of past accidents where people have stepped backwards, taking photographs and have disappeared down a mine shaft. I met one good lady in New Zealand, who had been confined to a wheel chair for the rest of her life after such an accident.

There are many cave dwellings, with smart abodes perhaps twenty feet below the surface, with air pumps on full time plus sewage devices. There is even a chapel and shops selling beautiful paintings as well as fine opal jewellery. On the surface, with not a blade in sight, there is a golf course with its 'greens', barren as the moon and a sign: "Keep off the Green"!

Adelaide to Tasmania

ADELAIDE WAS MY next stop. It has a most attractive square at its centre with rose red old fashioned buildings and side streets of vine clad single storey houses with shady verandas. I met a distant cousin, Alured Faunce, who is head of Probate and the son of the once owner of Sharstead Court near Sittingbourne, Kent, the Faunce stately home. He kindly gave up his time while we chatted. He was not amused when his father sold the house to the Wades, Virginia, the British tennis star's family, and spent the proceeds travelling the world for the rest of his life. Virginia started a tennis school there and it is good to know that the attractive building will be preserved in the future. Her parents lived in the old wing, with its attractive mellow bricks, while her brothers have the two wings and she has converted the stables for her own flat.

There are sixteen Faunce families in Australia, stemming from Captain Alured Faunce arriving in Sydney in 1832 to become a magistrate. He was accompanied by his brother Lieutenant Thomas Faunce. Dr Tom Faunce is a leading exponent of nano theory in Canberra. Another Doctor Faunce was Sydney's leading medical figure till he died in 2004. I met him and found him warm and friendly. With all these Australian members of my family, one might expect that permanent residency should have been possible. Even Citizenship!

After Adelaide there was the long drive through beautiful green farmland towards Melbourne. It was good to see flocks of sheep and healthy cattle after the skeletons in Northern Territory and Queensland. I stopped to see the 'Apostles', only eleven of them by then. They are thin pillars of red rock sticking up out of the sea, which is gradually eroding them.

Nearing Melbourne I spent a few days with Helen nee Blackbourn, Lester Robinson's wife and we climbed Mount Stirling together. She and Lester had an unusual glass walled house in eighty acres, surrounded by Bush and looking down on a distant lake. I hope the terrible fires have spared the house.

After the fires, I wrote to the Victorian Fire Commission and suggested they cut down all trees that could fall across roads, blocking people's escape routes. Also that they install the wartime air raid alarms that are not dependent on electricity and can be heard for miles. Again, that people are allowed to clear trees and scrub from around their houses as their lives are more important than trees, contrary to the belief of at least one local Council in that area.

Every house should have an escape bunker, excavated by a mechanical digger in ten minutes, and they either put a rectangular water tank on its side in the hole or build with concrete blocks, and have a fireproof door and steps leading down to the bunker. Fresh water and blankets should be installed. A little girl had survived the fire when she tripped into a wombat hole and the fire had passed over her, so such a bunker would surely save many lives. Air should be no problem as the fire travels fast.

The Commission welcomed my suggestions and I see bunkers are being built. There will always be bush fires as the debris from the gums trees requires frequent controlled burns and when there is a drought, such burns are impossible as there is no means of controlling them. It is refreshing to have ones suggestions accepted as people in high places tend to never acknowledge that other people's ideas have merit, possibly as they feel they should have thought of them first.

I returned to Melbourne and took off to Tasmania. Here I was wandering around an antique furniture shop and got talking to the owner. To my amazement he flourished his car keys and said to me, a complete stranger: 'Borrow my car for the day.' I rejected his kindness, saying that I would be afraid of having an accident but really appreciated his generosity.

I joined a tourist minicab group and we hurtled down to Port Arthur from Hobart. The countryside was lush with plenty of rain. The rain forests were beautiful with tall trees and creepers. We stopped at an animal sanctuary where we met the famous Tasmanian Devils. They are black, about forty five centimetres long and with barbarous teeth, which they use on each other out of pure devilment. We also stopped at a bridge made of huge logs and pretended to see the platypus, which our guide assured us was 'under that leaf.'

At Port Arthur, a beautiful spot with well-kept lawns and old prison cells, we went on a ghost hunt, but they were too shy to meet us. We learnt of the convict, who having escaped from prison with five others, kept himself alive by eating the others. No accounting for taste! He was caught and the authorities refused to believe him when he told them the truth. He was caught again later when trying to cross the causeway, which was policed by dog handlers.

On our return I managed to persuade the driver to reduce his speed to only frightening from crazy. It was just a couple of months later that a driver of a minibus crashed it in a nasty accident, driving too fast. I think I know the man!

We walked a long route to the lake by Cradle Mountain. It was through native Bush and very pleasant. An exhibitionist Polish lad tempted fate by standing on the edge of a cliff. We later drove up to the summit of Mount Wellington where the top was in brilliant sunlight, while the lower mountain was shrouded in thick cloud. There were some rather drunk golfers near us and I said, in a stage whisper: 'Wouldn't it be funny if they teed off into the clouds?'

The next thing, the golfers were pulling large rocks out of the way to establish driving room and they proceeded to tee off into the unknown. They got through many golf balls and I felt a twinge of guilt. Just imagine a romantic couple below the cloud, with golf balls 'snowing' around them!

After Tasmania, I left Australia for New Zealand, to spend eighteen glorious months there. Before leaving, I had nowhere to keep my precious Hyundai and sold it at a marked loss.

61

New Zealand, Land of the Long White Cloud

AFTER A HECTIC six weeks touring eastern Australia, often driving five to seven hundred km a day, I applied for a visa to visit New Zealand, where I still had good friends keeping in touch after forty years of silence. I was allowed to stay for six months, so being an optimist, I sent much of my furniture over there from England and I bought a nice house in Waipawa, Hawkes Bay. When the house next door came up for sale, it was only on the market for four hours before I bought it also and soon let it. So much cheaper than in the UK.

My own house had an acre and a half of flat land, a garage with its own shower, loo and wood burning stove and best of all, a swimming pool. The garage was so well equipped because the builder had built it before the house and had slept in the garage with his wife, while completing the house. This is a common practice in New Zealand but not allowed in Australia. Don't they like to legislate us out of existence!

Contrary to Aussie thinking, Hawkes Bay can and did get up to thirty five degrees centigrade. Drought stalked the hills while I lay, like Nero, in my own pool picking grapes from the vines festooning one end. There were three walnut trees, which provided a large wheelbarrow load every year; also a persimmon tree with its beautiful red fruit, and half a dozen apple trees. The Apricot tree only started to produce when I pruned it heavily and told it its days were numbered if it failed again. The twenty foot high avocado pear tree had one pear the year before I arrived and a horse ate it and died. I cut it down to size, about ten feet high and it continued to sulk. At least we were allowed to have bonfires for much of the year.

It was at Waipawa that I used up number six of my lives. I was in the main street when I felt really giddy. I made my way towards the doctor's surgery, leaning against the shops all the way along and passed out by my car, just across from the doctors. Feeling it coming on, I did a stage roll crumpling at the knees so I hit the tarmac fairly softly with the back of my head and only bled a little. Next thing I was being whisked flat out to the Hastings hospital forty miles away. They stuck needles into my stomach and I was beyond feeling much but they saved my life.

The second night I could not sleep as the nurses were having a high old time clanging things around in the room opposite the open door of my ward. When Derek the male nurse came in to stick me again, I asked very politely if the door might be shut. He replied very aggressively: 'You'd better get used to it.' And when he left, the door was still open. I must have been ill because I felt like planting him one but could not. Otherwise the nurses were fine and I owe them all my life.

On returning to Waipawa, I was to be on warfarin, or rat poison for the rest of my life. These essential little pills break up blood clots before they can cause a stroke. My South African doctor said to me: 'You ought to be dead. I can't understand it.' He repeated it every time we met after that. Wishful thinking? I saw the x-rays they took of me and there were clots everywhere. I guess he was right. I never recorded the sound of the ambulance. Damn!

Waipawa is a half-horse town. Probably the rear half. The only excitements are the new rugby team coached to great success by the pub owner, an ex All Black. It was fun on Saturdays seeing this well drilled side evolving from nothing and almost entirely Maori. The other event was hardly thrilling, the arrival of a Maori gang. They had not caused any trouble locally when I left but some would stride down the street eying one belligerently. I took a delight in staring them back equally hard, saying: 'G'day mate,' but I never had a reply.

I joined a Maori dance band and we played between Palmerston in the west and Gisborne in the north east, usually at RSL clubs, which have excellent and cheap meals most days. Keith was the lead singer. I played harmonica with a little sax to taste. It was great fun and we had large, appreciative audiences. At one Country and Western event, I teamed up with Dennis Marsh, a leading light in New Zealand and we had a great time. It was good to play again with a top voice.

Bob Huck and his wife, Enid came to live locally. He was a bee keeper and an ex potter. A large chain store put in a huge order for pots with Bob and then dropped out of it at the last moment, when he had made most of them. They decided to buy cheap from China. That is when he gave up pottery. We became good friends and I interviewed him for a short film about the Plymouth Blitz, which he observed as a small boy during the second World War. I added war sounds and it's not bad. He is now President of the local Slow Food club. He should go to the UK. There's plenty of that there!

While at Waipawa, I visited my old friends from Homewood, Bill and his lovely wife, Heather, near Napier, and Paddy Morrah with Helen and

Michael Morrah with Alison. It was wonderful to see them after such a long time and I was welcomed back as one of the family. The Kiwis are a warm hearted race and I treasure their friendship. Bill was one of an Insurance Company's victims, when short of money, they came over to Oceana promising fortunes to be made to gullible farmers and then made them sell most of their land to pay for the firm's bad debts.

I might tell the public at large how that firm failed to pay up on my son's legitimate claim, twice backed by the ombudsman and then took him to the cleaners. Just watch yourselves. I twice beat insurers when they tried to avoid paying my mother when she was twice hit by cars pulling onto the road on which she was travelling. They paid up in twenty four hours when I faced up to them. "I'll take you to the House of Lords if I have to." And I would have done. A little legal training can pay dividends.

62

Tempting Providence

DURING MY HAPPY time in Waipawa, I spent a year producing a documentary at Te Papa apple orchard, some five miles away. I filmed every aspect of the huge orchard, including from the air. I asked the pilot to take off the door so I could get clear vision and as he slid the plane on its side, I was dangling hundreds of feet up suspended by two straps. When the slipstream caught my camera, it was nearly jerked from my hands.

When I lost a screw from my tripod, one of the orchard mechanics measured another and then in twenty minutes had fashioned a perfect replica. Pretty impressive. They were a really pleasant and friendly crew. So helpful to a stray film maker, who was lurking with camera for a whole year, on and off.

I filmed the spraying, the pruning, the irrigation, bird-scarers, the anti-frost windmills, apple picking, grubbing out old trees, planting new ones, vehicle repairs and so on. Then I spent some days in the local apple packing shed, where they are washed, sized and even computerised with specimens being analysed. The Australian apple growers will do anything to keep New Zealand competitors out. In fact the apples sold to the public in New Zealand are usually of a higher quality than the Aussies' apples, with no blemishes or rot. Lower quality apples are kept for apple juice. Sorry guys but that is what I have seen and tasted. I filmed the crates of apples leaving the docks in Napier for Belgium, Germany and the UK. So from pip to ship.

I also made a twenty minute film around Napier, the Art Deco gem, which was destroyed in 1931 by an earthquake and fire. Several hectares of sea bed became dry land so the sea stopped flowing down Emison Street during very high tides. Now its Art Deco buildings are a great draw for tourists. I also filmed the air show and went up in an old Dakota, the workhorse of World War two, and also the long lunch where hundreds sit down to lunch on a train of tables near the sea front. They all dress up in period costumes of the Art Deco time, 1931 and are quite a sight.

There was also a super Shackleton flying boat that landed near me. They are beautiful relics from the past. Submarine hunters at one time. A six year old boy climbed up the mermaid statue and I took a charming clip of him talking to her. The atmosphere of Napier is pleasant and gentle, the only abrasive force, the sparrows spoiling my sound! I have also good footage of a steam train that I raced ahead of just north of Waipawa.

I visited South Island and found many comfortable bed and breakfasts for only about thirty five dollars. This was in 2003. I travelled around the island surprisingly fast under the impression that the speed limit was one hundred and forty km per hour. Te Anu was an experience as I spent ninety minutes in a light plane over the Southern Alps. Our five seater was perilously close to the mountains on both sides and we were only about thirty feet up as we emerged above a hanging valley. Down draughts were kind and we completed our trip over some of the sixteen hundred lakes in one piece. Six months later one of the pilots was killed and a year after that, the other one. It all adds weight to my hypothesis that Kiwi pilots are suicidal or manic.

I drove to Mount Cook, shrouded in dense cloud. I quickly filmed an ice cave and continued on to Queenstown. Taking a small ferry up Milford Sound we were lucky to be accompanied not only by dolphins but a two foot youngster feeding from its mum as it kept up with the boat at about two metres from my camcorder; the advantage of going in a smaller boat. We were only a metre out from the cliff face when our captain tried to get us wet from a waterfall. It rains here three hundred inches a year around the Sound, so waterfalls seldom dry up. I deliberately mix primary with metric to keep you on your toes. Some things seem easier to visualize in feet and inches.

I then drove on to Arrowtown, a little Historic village straight out of the Wild West with its single street of houses complete with verandas. I wandered off up the back and found a gold prospector bending over his sieve in the river. He was actually finding gold, not a fortune but about twenty dollars' worth a day. It was just his hobby but it made my day seeing the gold flakes in his pan. He told me the best place to find it is in the deep water on the outside of a bend in the river, where most gets deposited in a flood. Fine if you have a snorkel!

Then I walked across the river, only six inches deep in places. I walked up to the old gold diggings through scrub where no one had been for a long time, judging by the lack of paths. I found a blocked mine and old machinery but no large nuggets waiting to be picked up. Little fan tail birds perched on branches a couple of feet from my camcorder. They are so tame and have no reason to be scared of man. As I write this, my next task is to print today's young parrot's picture, sitting chatting to me a metre distant.

The Kiwis have a wonderful variety of exploits risking life and limb for adventurous tourists. They claim to have started bungee jumping, although the South American Indians may have first inspired them. You are strapped by the ankles and then leap into space above a river hoping that everything has been correctly assessed. Their aim is to have you pulled up by the elastic "rope" just short of the water but they got it wrong in a case I observed, where the jumper was partially emerged in the river and stripped of most of his clothes to the nervous laughter of us all. Eventually, when you stop bouncing, you are retrieved by a boat down below.

There is also white water rafting, which I filmed from a cliff top some hundred feet above. Along came the rafts and just as I had wished for, two overturned, tipping their entire crews into the water. There were bodies everywhere, all safe in their life jackets. It made a splendid series in my film. I did actually check that there were no fatalities, not being entirely cold blooded.

While filming I observed a man and his dog approaching near me. The man slid partially down the cliff, stopping some fifteen feet above the water. The dog watched his silly antics for a moment and then shaking his head, took off home. Perhaps he was used to his suicidal master.

There is also parachuting and hang-gliding. In fact a multitude of ways of reducing the population!

63

No Brakes!

I TOOK TO the road up the west coast of South Island and met three road/rail bridges, which stretch for at least two hundred yards. Cars have to give way to trains, but I wonder how many tourists realize that. I stopped and listened for a train before each bridge and survived. Near the north end of the island the main road turns east so I continued up north to find virgin territory, free from tourists, not that there were many.

There was a settlement with golf course and air strip. People working in the fields waved to me. I may have been the first car that day. On my way to Nelson and the return ferry my brakes gave out, just as I was having to cross a range of mountains. I stopped at the pedestrian rope bridge and filmed it swaying as others came on board. Then, my nerves no way improved, I set out to cross the mountains, using my gears as brakes. It was a hairy experience I have no wish to repeat. The road swings from one hairpin bend into the next incessantly through pine forests and steep slopes. The car company were quite casual when I explained what had happened.

The immigration office took most of a year to decide I could not stay in New Zealand, although I had lived there six years of my life. A Philippines immigrant with poor English told me that I would have to take an English test. I told her my family had lived in England the last five hundred years and I had taught English up to eighteen year-olds for thirty three years, so she backtracked. I had paid immigration lawyers thousands of dollars, making a case for me as a film maker, which she did not consider significant. (Last of The Mohicans and also the Twin Towers were being shot in New Zealand at that time) And so I had to go. When there was only one month left of my extended visa, she said, "Of course you can appeal." "How long will that take?" I asked her. "One month," she replied. I told her politely where to go. Two houses to sell! May she rot in Hell!

My neighbour in Waipawa, Graham Lawrence, kindly suggested I try Toowoomba, the garden city one hundred and thirty km inland from Brisbane as a possible place to settle. His sister lived there and he had enjoyed visiting her. So I hopped on a plane and flew across to Queensland, hired a car and drove up the two thousand feet to what I found as a perfect city. No chances of tsamis up there and less humidity than near the coast. It is also normally out of the cyclone area.

Toowoomba has ten cinema screens and the Empire theatre, which offers top stars like Kris Kristopherson and Nana Muscouri. It has over seventy clubs and there is so much to do there. So that is where I anchored. I have heard young people say that there is not enough going on in Toowoomba. Well, I have had to pull out of one of the two still camera clubs to make room for all my other activities. Leaving the Country Music club was as a result of a lack of participation. Pittsworth Country Club welcomed me but the road there at night is a fast track to the graveyard. A surface full of potholes, or it was. It has been repaired pretty well.

I am impressed by the Toowoomba pavements, in the centre of town, which all slope downwards to the roads. It is so considerate of the Council helping drunks feel they are walking upright! Rather like the Haggis, which has the left feet shorter than the right so goats can run round the mountain upright!

Australia would allow me to stay for four years at a time, although, not being Sudanese nor Somali, with a wife and six dependent children and hardly a word of English, I can never become a permanent resident, nor an Australian citizen. I do not even have the right to vote in local elections. At least they have just extended visas to ten years so with luck, I'll be dead before the next application has to be filed.

64

The Garden City of Toowoomba

MY FIRST DAY in Toowoomba I bought a car and a house, although I could not move in for six weeks. My guardian angels, Eleanor McGuigan and Yvonne Findlay allowed me to stay with them all that time. They were mutual friends with Richard and Rachel Martin of Windlesham House School. What a relief avoiding six weeks in a boring motel. Their constant good humour and toleration of the old man thrown in their midst was wonderful and we still indulge in witty repartee.

The car was a Mazda 323 and only three years old. It was a smooth drive, being automatic and has never let me down. The house had over half an acre of land and a large garden, which kept me busy. It had been built in 1975 and was partly on piles, one of which was on a slant. The possums would play football on the roof, which was inconsiderate of them, as I need my sleep. Opposite was a dance hall that held dances weekly and they carried on till twelve at night, so I was delighted when they went elsewhere with the arrival of Woolworths.

One day, before the advent of the Middle Ridge shopping centre, I saw the owner of the horses in the field opposite urging a boy on one of the horses to beat it more severely with a piece of plastic pipe. I strode across to remonstrate with the Irishman and told him it was the best way to spoil a horse. He retorted that the horse was already spoilt. I have used the incident in one of my horror scripts, where the man is dragged by one stirrup through mud, rocks and nettles. Wishful thinking!

I soon joined a walkers' group, led by the incredible old Dutchman, Bill, and waded through the Bush once a week for five years till my hip forbade it. They are still a wonderfully friendly and cheerful crowd and visit my house as a resting place where they can eat their lunches and tell me their exploits. It is great to have their company.

I also joined the Jazz club where the Windy City group plus invaders from Brisbane like Caxton Street, play rousing Jazz. The late Denis Levonis, the originator of Windy City, taught me to play by music and my clarinet playing leapt forwards. All my life, prior to this, I had listened to a tune and then played it, a useful gift. But being able to read the dots opens up another dimension. I shall always be grateful to Denis for his lucid instructions.

A natural place for meeting people in Toowoomba is the Rendez-Vous Café in Ruthven Street. Tony Wigan, a volunteer announcer come host on the local radio makes everyone feel as if they are his long lost friends. He made much of my abortive visit to the "Old Country" and ambushed me with the local paper, The Chronicle, who treated me like a cross between the village idiot and a local star. At least I got a reasonable photo of myself to put on the Net. Like other strays, I visited the café twice a week for a decent meal complete with salad and we joked our way along, giving Tony as good as he doles out. He has recently sold the café.

One day, while at the Toowoomba Show, I asked Pat Menz, Chairman of the Toowoomba Folk Club, if I could join him. This started a duo that was to last till I left Australia. I was listening to a solo artist playing and singing at Preston Peak Winery and asked him if I could sit in with him for a song or two. We played for over an hour and as we finished a woman came up and asked me whether I would consider playing at another winery, The Wedge-tail, at Kingsthorpe. I replied that she should ask the other guy as he was the entertainer there. She said: "No, it is you we want," so that was the start of eighteen months playing at The Wedge-tail, first a couple of times with Mal Rainbow, the brilliant pianist, then with Pat, every weekend apart from six, prevented by rain. We only stopped when petrol price rises suffocated our audiences.

Then we played all over like three times one year at Jondaryan Woolshed, The Manley Hotel in Brisbane, six times a year at Pitsworth for the elderly, for the Carnival of Flowers in Toowoomba and others. Laidley was always a favourite with appreciative audiences. Well, it was till the floods.

The other day Sam from Rudd's historic pub in Nobby asked me over to play for fifty bus passengers on my own. It was the most appreciative audience of my life, and he paid me 50% more as a bonus. The meals there are superb and the regalia on the walls, absorbing. They even bought two of my books.

We had to let one musical colleague go because people said he was pulling us down. He announced proudly that he had never practised in his life and did not even take the hint when I said that if he started now, he might improve. Some you just cannot help! He was also an inveterate smoker and his hacking cough was not endearing to the audience. The last straw for me was when he coughed violently and his false teeth flew across the stage! He died of course.

Some audiences seemed hard to please. At a veteran car rally we played for nearly three hours, giving of our best. No one bothered to clap once. As we were gathering up our equipment, quite a task, one of the audience said how much they had enjoyed the music. No comment! It does seem a Queensland trait, that one should ration applause. Having said that, one night they applauded Greg the Piano and me after every song.

65

Teaching Immigrants

As if there were not enough to do, I taught Sudanese immigrants on a voluntary basis. They were aged from about sixteen to thirty in the centre, TRAMS, by the Catholic Church in Toowoomba for a year, helping students with their homework and others. There was no continuity or contact with their schools so one could not have made much of a lasting impact. I finally used the subjects I learnt for my degree, such as Law, Economics and History, even the History of Art and Religion from the Bible. Also English and Maths. I finally stopped when faced with a young lady with six children and another on the way, who did not even know the alphabet. And they want more immigrants here?

Perhaps they should make sure they and the indigenous races actually work, first. One hears of families where three generations have lived off the state, with no intention of working. Others claim benefit on the shakiest of reasons. It is time the politicians woke up to the potential on their doorstep. No work, no pay!

It is amusing if not frightening how the councils and state government are so cavalier with our limited resources. We almost run out of water and our roads are thick with traffic, so they temporarily solve the water problem and then encourage more people to reside in Queensland. We already have to import much of our food, so they allow the best farming land to be destroyed for more coal, so it can be sold to destroy more of the atmosphere. No one speaks of the need to control population growth so it continues to explode and then surprise, surprise, the millions starving also increase. Have your brain removed and then you are fit to lead the countries or the world.

The Flexi School Films

We of the Darling Downs Moviemakers were asked by Glen Postle, a lecturer from the USQ university to make three films of different lengths about the Flexi School. Bernie Moore made a very long and expert historical version, Bob Cheeseman made a short film and I made a twenty minute film for Glen to use when talking to groups about the school.

Flexi school is for children of about fifteen plus, who have dropped out of the main school system. There are about eighty youngsters there and they have a very flexible lesson structure. I only observed a computer class and a social studies class in action but there are other subjects taught. The main aim is to get the children up to a standard of numeracy and literacy so that they can achieve employment. They improve their social skills, a very real need in some cases, where they have become hostile to conventional values.

The causes for their rejection of mainstream schools includes some sort of abuse at home, or dysfunctional families, where they have no support. Sometimes a child is born rebellious and that's a fact! Whatever the reasons, it is essential that this wide problem is addressed and such youngsters are catered for.

They visit a local sports centre where I filmed kick boxing and basketball. They have a skate board arena next to the school, and there is a drum kit, a keyboard and guitars in the music area. The school is fulfilling a serious need and has a waiting list. It would be most helpful to society to have flexi schools in every town. Often these are bright children, whose brains are needed by society. The converse, if they feel rejected and enter the world of drugs or crime, would be a running cost for the tax payers. It is cheaper to send someone to Eton, one of England's leading Public (Private) Schools, than to keep them in prison. A sobering thought.

Flexi school improves social skills and assists self-confidence to grow. It is one of the most valuable creations I have met. So why not more of them?

66

The Fine Cotton Scam 1984

I WAS SITTING at my computer minding my own business when there was a knock on the door. I opened it to find a Jaguar parked in my driveway. The driver introduced himself as John Gillespie and he had a friend with him. John had heard in New South Wales of this screen writer in Toowoomba and had driven up the three hour journey on the off chance of meeting me.

John Gillespie wanted me to write a full feature film script to be called "The Man Called The Phantom," a biography about him and his involvement in the biggest horse racing scam in Australia's history. He paid me a small fee, with the rights to half his proceeds if the film ever got made. The story included him as a young boxer being engaged by a leading bookmaker in wheeling and dealing with race horses. He switched horses having spread bets round the world with the bookmaker and the long and the short of it was that another bookmaker was taken for over fourteen million dollars, which was lot of money in 1984. John was paid nearly two million dollars for his part and he served a four months sentence in prison for his pains but laughed all his way to the bank when he came out and the police failed to trace his ill-gotten gains when he sought refuge in America.

John bought a chain of bars in Malaya and brought racing mares over there from Australia. A local man offered him five thousand dollars each, when they were worth six times that, and threatened him when he refused. A friendly local took John's part and the first man met with a fatal accident. Anyhow it is a rattling good story and would make an excellent film with my exciting screenplay. I believe John is still looking for a producer and may he succeed as I worked hard on that script. For the present the film is on hold since a criminal is not allowed to benefit from the spoils of his crime.

John has an autistic son and he asked me to visit his boy's school and play an instrument and tell a story or two, so I did and before I visited them, I wrote this little poem for the boy:

My World

Please don't laugh at me
Because I can't talk like you.
I feel your jeers, I have my fears
Trapped in my world.

Swimming in a goldfish bowl
Can't make them understand.
We speak our words but like the birds
Soar in another land.

Take us for what we are,
Children from another star.
Speaking foreign tongues, same heart, same lungs.
Trapped in your world.

How the tension swells
Trying to communicate.
Perhaps one day to work and play
Free in your world.

67

Music – Kelly's Armour

PAT MENZ PLAYS a steel guitar, a normal wooden one and a banjo. He has improved his singing as he is more relaxed and strains his vocal cords less by my taking solos. He is particularly fond of lengthy political songs. We have played together for about six years and meld pretty well. We play a lot of sixties and seventies tunes plus Country and Folk. I throw in a little Latin and even Glenn Miller and Calypso. Also the occasional music from the Shows and light Opera.

Pat and I play some of our gigs free of charge, especially for old folk. I only ask enough to pay for my various instruments and replacements. Harmonicas blow out frequently and the clarinet has to be serviced every two years. The sax cost hundreds of dollars to be re-padded. One member of the Darling Downs Moviemakers listened to us for some time in the Carnival of Flowers and said: "Hey Mike, you really can play!" It is funny how people never think that people they know can be any good at anything. A prophet in his own county syndrome. Paul Spencer gave me a nice little DVD he made of us playing at the 150 years Toowoomba celebrations last year at the station. It includes a steam train that is far better looking than me.

One double gig took place in Dalby, when we played for five hours plus on each of two consecutive nights and then motored home, to arrive at one thirty and one o'clock at night. Musicians earn their money. Three farmers bought CD's off us at give-away prices, just to clear the deck.

We have some excellent world stars visit us in Toowoomba. I enjoyed Glen Campbell at Rumours Night Club. His guitar playing is out of this world. Then Foster and Allen have just visited yet again and created a lovely evening.

I have mentioned playing with Greg the Piano, Kruger. We played for nine hours with only half an hour break, at Nobby Historic pub, or "Rudd's Pub", half an hour south of Toowoomba off the Warwick road. We had originally met there when I joined him and later looked round to find the room in which we were playing, was packed with listeners. This was before I went back to the UK in December 2009. This pub is well worth a visit, especially when we are playing there! The food is excellent and the menu wide. It is best to book ahead as they are often sold out, in spite of having a large dining area.

68

Back to Frozen UK

IT HAD BEEN very hot and we had dust storms thrown in for good measure. There is to be a coal mine opened up within twenty miles of Toowoomba and as I am allergic to coal dust, I thought it was time to leave. The exchange rate was very much in my favour, so I sold my house for a handsome profit and escaped the traffic and other delights brought by the Woolworths development across the road. I arrived in the UK with all my furniture to follow, courtesy of the ever efficient Pickfords. My furniture is arguably the best travelled in the world. Well one has to entertain the natives somehow.

I arrived in the worst winter since 1962 and found an inch of ice covering my car, when staying with Tim in Reigate. Entrance and exit roads from the motorway were closed. The country was at a standstill, frozen solid, with only seven degrees of frost in the south but twenty in the north. Airports were closed. It was grim. I spent a very happy Christmas with Tim, Christopher, who lived nearby in Godstone, and Caroline, who had beaten the snow on the motorway from Lancashire.

I managed to drive across to my sister Wendy and her husband John Prescott in Essex. They live in a delightful thatched cottage, to which they have added sympathetically and we had a cheerful three days before the threat of snow drove me westwards once more. Wendy said I was quite mad coming back at this time of the year. I strongly disagreed. Just imagine arriving in summer and then having such a winter, being committed, house bought and furniture having arrived. At least mine was able to do a skid turn, having been too stormy to land for three weeks and return to Australia without Customs or unpacking.

Wendy and John had met on the SS Nevasa on which he was the purser and she the matron. They married and bought a pub near Penrith at the highest part of the main road north to Scotland, so it was the first to be cut by snow every year. When they took over their pub it had a handful of patrons, but such was their hospitality and cooking prowess, it became a great success. John's old sea comrades used to have reunions there too.

Almost opposite were the ruins of a huge stately home, still inhabited by a fine statue. The windows had been boarded up on the introduction of the window tax and now the roof had caved in. What a waste!

I had hoped to visit my sister Elizabeth but needed to know if she was working or at home, and exactly where she and her partner, Adrian live. They have bought a barn, which Adrian has partly done up, with exotic Italian tiles and other nice touches. He makes his living from constructing super furniture and yet they have to ascend a ladder to their bedroom. I find this strange since he made his parents a stairway which would not be out of place in a stately home. They live rather like Victorians of perhaps 1850. There is no electricity. Imagine being without a fridge!

No electricity so how does she charge her mobile phone I gave her? Not often! No drainage. Say no more! They raise their own vegetables on about an acre plus and being in Somerset, there should be no shortage of rain water. Well, it is their choice but not for me! Elizabeth is good with horses and had a job walking out some for a local man. I never got to see them on that trip with impossible roads.

The weather relented enough for me to drive carefully down to Dorset after Christmas, where I had chosen to buy a house. Dorset has the best sunshine and rainfall figures in Britain and a reputation for live music in its pubs. So I chased houses for two freezing weeks. Finding estate agents open and accommodation during the three weeks around Christmas and the New Year in the UK is near to impossible. Whenever I found a house worth looking at, it was either shrouded in fog or as in one case, stated by the agent to have solar panels, when it was patently obvious it had none. One house was pleasant but almost opposite a closed down turkey factory, so what new horror would be opened shortly? Another was idyllic but sure to be cut off with a little snow or frost, as it snuggled in a deep valley miles from the madding crowd in a forgotten hamlet.

I did find an ex farm house with copious outbuildings and eight acres of good flat land but my alert daughter Caroline noticed that its construction consisted of very thin walls and I should have had to spend a fortune on rebuilding. The owner expected the buyer to take on half a dozen hens as part of the deal. I would have gladly done so, ensured of my breakfasts! The flat land would have been ideal to land my helicopter when my film scripts sell and make a fortune!

The search was enhanced by such cold weather that I resorted to day long pub crawls, seeking hot coffee to thaw out my body. Parking was both expensive and hard to find. In the evenings I trudged round the pubs discovering live "music", if that is what you call the noise at a level of Concord's engines. The final straw was when I was encouraged to join one group, who then allowed a banshee woman to screech like a cat with its... caught in the mangle. She went on and on and I left. The audience thought she was terrific. Gawd!

One land lady gave me a tiny electric fire, which might have raised the temperature of my bedroom one degree, while the shower room was Arctic. Only the polar bears were missing. The landlady mentioned, as I was leaving, that she had forgotten to turn on the night storage heater. I could have told her that but thought it was broken. She surely noticed the temperature of my room? Finally I found the Well Inn on the north side of Bridport, half a mile from the glacier. It was comfortable and warm although I noticed the temperature fading after breakfast. But the cooked breakfasts were generous and the couple who ran it were friendly.

Why did I stay in Dorset and not retreat to Tim's warm flat? Firstly, I felt guilty that he had given me his bedroom while he slept in his sitting room on a mattress and secondly I was conscious that at each possible house I had visited, I met the same potential buyers, and there was very little presentable property under four hundred thousand pounds for a three bedroom house. One of those would be for an office. So remain in Dorset and freeze but with a chance of success.

Another winter has arrived in Europe, the worst ever since statistics have been kept, we are told. Thank goodness I did not buy a house there. They are too young to remember 1947!

69

The Joys Of Air Travel & To China

AFTER A MONTH of misery – I had an infected lung – Tim managed to drive me to the airport. I got out of Heathrow, Gatwick airport being closed, after an abortive attempt, where the QUANTAS plane was iced up and the busiest airport in the world had insufficient de-icers. I did notice the Virgin Airways plane beside us managed to fly! We waited for an hour and a half and then taxied to the runway only after a long wait there, to be told we had missed our slot and had to be de-iced again. So, after a total wait in the plane, of three hours, we were airborne. But there was worse: Within eight metres of my seat were three infants. They took it in turns to bawl all the twelve hours till Singapore. One had a really angry cry. I would not like to meet him on a dark night!

Surely it would be possible to have infant free planes? I would willingly pay extra for a quiet flight. I thankfully ejected myself from my flight companions and spent a couple of nights in Singapore. The family, who talked virtually all night on my second night in the hotel and kept me awake, are on my hit list. I was feeling so crook that next day I had to force myself to look round a little part of the city. I thought: "I am never going to fly again, so I had better get my money's worth." So I staggered to the short queue for the Giant Eye, the replica of the London version, which wheels you up a couple of hundred feet into the sky to look down on the human ants below. It was a pleasurable experience and one I should remember always.

I entered my plane home for the last leg of the journey and imagine my delight when there, six yards away from my seat, was the angry baby. He did not disappoint in the last eight hours nor let up. There were a little boy and girl even closer to me, who were delightful, hardly making a sound the whole way. So much for air travel. Never again. Funny, it never happened so badly with Singapore Airways. Perhaps their attentive and caring staff help relax everyone.

Back in warm Australia, I stayed again with Eleanor and Yvonne, plus Eleanor's daughter, Sarah and her eight year old son, Josh. Home from home! I bought a Mazda 3 Sports with leather upholstery and a 2.4 litre engine, which responds very quickly and has cruise control – magnificent on a long run. Its all round disc brakes are most effective too.

After some heavy searching, I found a four bedroom house, with an office and great entertainment area, again on Middle Ridge but away from traffic and with a more manageable garden. So all has worked out admirably. The exchange rate changed radically in my favour again when returning from England, which virtually paid for the trip and furniture moving, which would have had to happen in moving to a better house in any case.

From Beijing to Helsinki: Two years ago I had flown with Tour Directors to Beijing, where we feasted in our smart hotel before exploring the Silk Market, where some of our party bargained for exotic garments or cheap DVD's. We entered Red Square of infamous repute when the student faced off a column of tanks, and we saw the huge picture of Chairman Mao, instigator of the time when intellectuals, and the professional classes were forced to work as labourers planting rice for their sins of teaching the Chinese work force and doctoring their needs. Tripods were not allowed in Red Square and we were hurried on. A dangerous weapon?

We visited the Great Wall of China, and most of us climbed the sixteen hundred steps to the top, not doing my hip any good. Building was started in the 7th century BC but failed to keep out the Mongols, in spite of being defended by a million troops. It had better luck with the rabbits, according to the advertisement. We were served an excellent meal up there. It had come up on the cable car. The views were wonderful and we learnt that it was known as the largest and longest cemetery in the world as when many builders died, they were buried under the three thousand mile wall.

China has this inspired idea of making its prisoners work in prison factories – and how can the rest of the world compete with free labour unless they follow suit – and when they leave they are used to working and may also have a trade.

I had heard that Beijing was a city of bicycles but such is the new wave of prosperity, you see very few. However the streets are jammed with new cars. We had rides in sedan chairs over the old cobbled streets and visited a market full of fresh vegetables, fish and meat. There was a visit to an enamel shop with a display of countless gorgeous jars and dishes decorated ornately with all the colours under the sun. Also to a silk mat factory where one mat of only two feet wide by four feet long took many months to make, the intricate patterns painstakingly copied frequently by a young girl. They could be bought for thousands of dollars. I mean the mats!

We were treated to an ethereal vision of dance and acrobatics, the participants diving backwards through hoops, among many other displays, at the

Beijing Opera House. The ghostly quality of the music and swirling birdlike and dragon people in magnificent costumes belonged to a different world. Filming and photography were not allowed, as was apparent by the ceaseless flashing so I filmed with the rest from a front seat concealing my camcorder under a napkin. So many spinning plates with three layers of acrobats standing above each other, made me wonder what happened if one was broken in practice? Did they have to do the washing up for a week?

The Forbidden City revealed that the Emperor had three thousand concubines, well not all at once, and the Mongols had failed to enter his palace when they took the city in 1900.

Mongolia: After the many concerts we attended in Beijing and their wonderful acrobats and dancers, we took the Trans-Siberian Express to Mongolia, the remote horse bound country, which has opened its borders to tourists. We were shown around the Lotus Orphanage, in Ulaanbaatar, started by its current manager, Didi Kaletia, an American tourist, who could not bear to see the starving children on the streets. The children, about one hundred of all ages, are well fed, clothed and educated. They have little help from the government, which reflects hearts of stone or maybe just acute poverty as a nation. We heard them singing most professionally and watched a gym display. They were joyful but well-disciplined and should grow into model citizens. If any of my readers feel like contributing any sum, however small, I can channel it straight to the orphanage, with no middle rake-offs. It seemed so worthwhile, I have contributed a fair sum.

We visited a monastery in the town and heard of the persecution of monks in the past, when under communist government. The prayer wheels were spinning frequently. We left the capital, Ulaanbaatar, with its many horse statues and huge central square and journeyed across a barren plain to a settlement.

In the evening we were treated to some warm wine and sat around a bonfire singing. It was very pleasant and the natives sang a beautiful and haunting melody.

We slept for two nights in the round tents, gers, heated by wood fires, which were stoked up every three hours through the night. A woman would enter to put fresh wood on the stoves and we roasted for an hour, then were comfortable for an hour and then cooled off for the last hour.

Next morning some of the party rode the stocky little ponies favoured by the natives. Others were pulled along in an ox cart. We visited a Shaman place of worship where blue rags marked where donations had been left to the witch doctors. I lost several kilograms choosing to miss much of the evening meals, in favour of filming the dancers and singers. A shaman danced for us, swirling in loose garments and four musicians played balalaika type instruments very well; also a violin like instrument. A contortionist showed us her way of preventing obesity. Was the human body really designed for the head to bend back and appear between the legs? The Shaman is like a witch doctor and heals the believers. They still operate in the north of Mongolia, a vestige of faith healing.

The last day we visited a nomad's family and watched him lasso a pony at the gallop. Modern methods were indicated by a light motorbike propped outside their tent. The tents can be packed up ready to go in three quarters of an hour. The family were burnt brown by the sun and wind. Their pleasant features were smiley and friendly. They treated us to a meal and I took refuge from their mare's milk in my filming. The nomads are the only inhabitants of the plains and dependent largely on the horses they raise and sell. They are a free people and protected to a degree by the government. Tourism must be a useful new form of income. Altogether the Mongolian trip was pleasant and educational as we met a totally different civilization.

We were bussed back to Ulaanbaatar along the very bumpy mud roads and stretched our legs at an enormous gold painted statue before re-embarking on the train once more. The rail track led through featureless plains, lakes, rocky gullies and through fields, which appear to be sown with blue plastic bags. They stretched for miles and there had to be millions of them. Did they really think they would grow to produce more bags?

70

Trans-Siberian "Express"

THE BORDER TRANSFER to Russian tracks necessitated the train being jacked up and lowered onto different gauge tracks. It took place in the early hours and was fascinating to watch as the train was inched up so slowly you hardly noticed the movement. The whole drawn out process would have been avoided if we had simply transferred to a Russian train, but is this too simple? We had our passports and visas checked, which also took many hours. Did they really report back to Moscow to see whether Putin approved of each of us?

The train eventually moved on and we nestled back on our bunks to sleep. Next day we found we had no restaurant car so we drew in our belts till an occasional station appeared. We were never sure how long the train would stop at a station, usually between fifteen and thirty minutes. One unfortunate Russian passenger was left behind and goodness knows when the next train would arrive.

I had been warned of such likely events and had a couple of soup packets, which lasted a day each, two cups plus an indifferent sausage snatched at a ten minute halt. If anyone wants to lose weight, travel Trans-Siberian.

At one station a small boy with an exquisite smile was selling hand painted pictures and postcards. He took exception to my filming them and showed quite a temper.

At another station there was a tall statue of the first Mongolian astronaut. I did not know he existed; also a youth brass band, which had been travelling on the train. They gave an impromptu concert of quite a high standard, and I like the footage I shot; very tuneful.

I was lucky to have a four birth compartment only having to share with our tour leader and so avoided the drunken Russian hulk next door. The joys of the Trans-Siberian Express!

Having survived two days without, we were treated to a restaurant car, complete with heavily smoking Russians and tiny helpings. The next three days I could have dispensed with. The endless Russian steppes have little attraction and it was with considerable relief that we entered Siberia.

Siberian Culture: We disembarked at the capital, Irkutsk and admired the "Paris" of Russia. The architecture is attractive with fresh pastel colours and stately buildings. It was very different from the mining area, where dissidents were sent in Stalin's time. There are many churches with appealing bells ringing out their Sunday changes. (Forgive the pun.) An occasional log cabin reminds one of poorer days.

We visited Lake Baikal, the largest fresh water lake in the world. The temperature never rises above two degrees centigrade. One of our party, crazy for attention, stripped off and dived into the lake. He was in the near freezing water for about a minute before striding to shore and his towel. He made his point having almost lost it! We passed an uncompleted hotel, a common enough sight since Gorbachev brought in Perestroika with dire financial consequences. There was a busy street market with locals and the odd tourist searching among the leather goods and souvenirs.

On our return to Irkutsk I discovered a pan pipe player of rare talent. Its haunting melodies reminded me of Georgi Zamphire, a lifetime ago. In fact I carefully checked to ensure he was really playing. I treasure his CD.

We visited the opulent house of a dissident successful general, Prince Volensky, who had been sent to Siberia, without his wife and children. After some years surviving the mines and working in the fields, he was granted a pardon and lived in style with other dissidents, creating a cultural centre. We listened to some fine piano playing and singing before being refreshed with sherry; it was all very civilized.

Having enjoyed our Siberian interlude, we set off for Moscow. The city had changed a little in the fifty years since my last visit. The eight lane highways in each direction had become as congested as London or Brisbane. The city had had a face lift with some most attractive architecture. We visited the dock where the battleship in 1917 had fired a blank to begin the revolution, which deposed the Czar and led to the murder of all his family and their unfortunate servants. We had concerts every night and slept in a very comfortable hotel.

We had a river trip along the Volga and passed the Kremlin where Putin had his office. We were serenaded by busty women and an accordion playing vigorous dances, which my fellow travellers joined in, while I filmed the sunbathers on the river banks.

One day we lunched in what had been a rich merchant's house, with ornate fittings and a loo which amused us all with mirrors for all its walls in a gold and green hue. We also had a day concert in a restaurant with a trio playing, one a bass balalaika, which he was clearly enjoying and a girl on some strange but similar instrument. Her fingers were a blur, too fast to follow. A well-endowed Russian matron sang lustily and it was all of a very high standard. I missed most of my meal but love the music I captured. One can eat any time!

St Petersburg – once Leningrad

Eventually we set off for St Petersburg, Putin's favourite city. It had been seriously shelled in World War 2 but Hitler's mob never managed to take the city. The Hermitage museum, surely the finest in the world, had its treasures hidden in case of Nazi intrusion. Some went to the Urals for safety. The Germans were infamous for pillaging Art treasures in every country they invaded. Three thousand windows had been broken in the fighting. The people were starving and ate grass and bark.

We were shown around the museum by our guide at breakneck speed and I frequently incurred her displeasure by getting lost accidentally on purpose, to the extent that the rest of our party were skated past a wonderful gallery of sculptures, which I filmed in their absence. I nearly fought World War Three when a hostile caretaker told me I could not film in one gallery. I did anyhow and dared her to prevent me. Having paid so much and having travelled so far, no one was going to stop me filming. Another concierge was asleep at her post.

It was wonderful to see paintings, jewellery, furniture and sculpture by the world's most famous and accomplished experts. Michael Angelo, Da Vinci, Monet, Picasso, Van Gogh and the rest. It would take a week to do justice to the museum, and it was very hard to shoot good film footage while being jostled by thrusting crowds but Denis and Peggy Levonis said they had watched my film of the museum three times, so it was worthwhile.

We visited St Isaac's Cathedral with its superb green malachite columns. Its cross is decorated with one hundred kilograms of gold. It was designed by a young Parisian architect, Auguste Richard de Montferrand. He died a month after its consecration in 1858. Czar Nicholas' family, the Romanovs' remains are buried there. There is room for fourteen thousand people standing to attend services there. It is now a museum but church services are held there on special occasions.

There was also the Church of the Spilled Blood, built on the site where Tsar Alexander II was assassinated. There were many beautiful biblical paintings on the walls and ceilings. The Bolsheviks wanted to dismantle it in 1940 but Hitler's blockade gave them other things to think about. In the sixties they wanted to again but it was preserved first as a storage depot, then as a museum.

We saw the Astoria hotel where Hitler intended to celebrate his taking of St Petersburg, but he failed. If he had an ounce of sense, he would have learnt from Napoleon's defeat and not lost a whole army. The pavement artists reminded one of Hyde Park corner in London.

Leaving the picturesque St Petersburg, we were grateful for only a day and a half train journey to Helsinki. Finland has lost much of its territory to Russia. Its capital shows Russian influence by way of its architecture. I was impressed by its church part built into a rock, but most worthy of note were the total lack of obese people. The rest of the world should ask how they do it. Also, the Finns all speak good English, and seemed a very pleasant and civilized people. They had a huge ferry in port but being a weekend it was very quiet. A comfortable hotel was our base, till we flew back to Australia, a journey of some forty hours. Many thanks to Tour Directors for a most memorable trip.

71

Other Films I Have Made

WHILE IN MY first house in Toowoomba, I had charming neighbours and took advantage to use them for a short film, "Late At Night". I had the parents going out for the evening and leaving their dear ten year-old, Andrew alone but for a sick elder sister, Annie. A burglar arrives and ties up Andrew, who unties himself and tricks the burglar into the walk-in airing cupboard. When he slams the door, the burglar finds there is no handle on the inside of the door. When his parents return home, they are convinced Andrew has been dreaming, when he tells them he has captured a real live burglar. It is not a bad ten minute film and gave us all some amusement.

I filmed the Aborigine initiation site near Highfield north of Toowoomba with its caretaker, Brian. I have called it: "Reflections". There is now an Education Centre here and they invite school visits to see the stone rings in the paddock and hear how over a thousand tribesmen would visit once a year for the initiation rites of their young boys. Didn't the girls get in on the act! People would first visit the Bunya Mountains for the nuts. There is not a huge amount to see but Brian has dug up various rocks and there are revealed shapes of an emu, a tortoise and a fish, the tokens of different tribes. He has lent me an unpublished book of the life of the early settlers.

Before the white man invaded with his flu, smallpox and other killing diseases, the indigenous people had their own laws, medicine and customs, which had been handed down over thousands of years. Treated as having no rights in their own land must been hard to swallow, but that has also been the fate of most nations. The Normans treated the Saxons in England as slaves and the Romans were not much better.

A fighter pilot from World War 2, Ben Gilbert, the current owner of that land, has given back the Initiation site to its people, a generous gesture it is hoped they appreciate.

In this documentary I have also filmed the local clay pits, where huge numbers of bricks were made and the aboriginals got their face painting colours. I included Donna's indigenous products shop that used to be near Toowoomba station. The film may be of interest to some.

The Darling Down Movie Makers, to whom I belong, have filmed Pat and me playing at the Jondaryan Woolshed Brunch and I have added various cutaways depicting the many activities they have there. Jondaryan, about forty minutes from Toowoomba, is a large Historic centre with working blacksmith, water bore driller and even a model train for the kids to ride on. It has every sort of vintage steam engine. This DVD is about forty five minutes long, although the original was over ninety minutes.

The Movie Club with its vigorous chairman, Don Herrmann, has provided nine cameramen to film a motorbike ride for Cancer. We took up our various positions over nearly two hundred km of countryside and moved on to fresh positions ahead of the motorbikes twice when they stopped for lunch and a break. They were led by a policeman at a goodly pace. We raised about twenty six thousand dollars over all, and our DVD helped in the process. I had my final position filming the bikes coming into Toowoomba and received some dirty looks from the public, who obviously thought I was a "snooper" of some sort. The bike run has become an annual event.

I also filmed a Bush farm north of Crow's Nest in Queensland and hoped to see a "dingo howler". He howls in the early morning to attract dingoes so he can shoot them. The dingo will attack and kill quite large cows, and their calves are fair game. They tear them apart and eat them while still alive. Any child in the vicinity is very much at risk of sharing the same fate.

Bob, whose farm it is, told me the wonderful account of how they had a crocodile in their dam, which effectively stopped the four children from drowning themselves. Crocs have their uses. Before you go out and buy one, remember they grow to eighteen feet or more in length, are virtually indestructible and eat children and adults.

One full feature film script I have high hopes for is "Try And Stop Us". It is based loosely on the actual event after the fall of Singapore to the Japs in 1942, when four Aussies and Kiwis travelled the three thousand miles from Singapore to Australia through jungle and over the sea. My story has a couple of beautiful girls escaping with them and their ambushing a Jap patrol. They also destroy an air-field and shoot up a stick of paratroopers, who are fair game as they descend.

They are captured and escape, helped by the Malaysian boy, whom they have taken under their wing when his mum was shot by the Japs. They blow up a Jap motor torpedo boat with Molotov cocktails and survive a horrendous storm. There is a touch of romance and some betrayal. It should make a huge film with worldwide appeal. Someone will make a load of money out of it, I hope while I am still alive to see it. The budget is under $5 million, a snip compared to what Hollywood spends. Updating, a Gold Coast producer and director have optioned it, giving them the right to make the film over the next year. They have had a reading with the actors, who loved the script. So perhaps there is light at the end of the tunnel.

72

Botswana

LATE IN 2007 I took a photographic trip to Botswana with a South African couple, a vociferous Aussie and three Americans. The latter hardly talked to anyone outside their circle for the whole twelve days on the trip. We landed at Johannesburg, the crime centre of South Africa, if not the world. We were not allowed to walk the two hundred yards from the hotel with its high spiked fence and electric gate to a restaurant. It would be too dangerous. I had not been able to take my decent tripod as we had been warned that anything valuable would be stolen at the airport.

Next day we flew to Botswana, the third largest diamond producing country in the world. They are a most enlightened people and have very little crime. There is free education till seventeen and it was interesting hearing our native camp workers conversing in Oxford English. They are often taught by teachers from the best schools in England. The chief had been married to an English woman when they became independent from Britain and he listened to her ideas.

We travelled by boat up the Okavango delta and admired the lilies and other plant life. An elephant cooling in the water looked as if it might charge these intruders breaking into its ablutions. There are one hundred and twenty thousand elephants wandering around those parts including Zimbabwe, Tanzania and others. They need culling as they are eating themselves out of existence. We saw plenty of evidence in the stripped trees dying all over. (And one hears the "experts" on television talking about the need to protect the elephants – an endangered species!)

Our days were spent filming exotic birds, hippos with their huge mouths and even larger behinds, crocodiles with their evil grins as they contemplate having a photographer for desert, and the South African girl would have tasted delicious. There was a five foot long monitor, and wart hogs. The giraffes ambled close by and a lion strolled past our open sided land-rover, not noticing our presence, barely four feet away. Our guide whispered as the lion approached: "Don't move. Freeze". We later observed their ambush late one evening being set up for some buffalo.

Evenings were very civilized as we stopped at sun down religiously for the essential gin and tonic, or wine for the less discriminating. Our dinners were excellent and there was wine laid on, as much as you wanted. One evening we were delighted to have a leopard join us for the first course but it slunk away before we could get our cameras out.

There are said to be only about four hundred and sixty leopards ranging free in the world. So imagine my delight when having failed to see one in daylight, I asked the guide of another group if he had seen any around. He told us of one quite near. We found it up a tree, casually washing itself. The force eight gale swayed my cheap tripod around but I have some respectable footage of the big cat staring down my lens from thirty yards away. Having washed itself from tip of tail to ears, it stood up making a wonderful Jungle Book silhouette and then prowled down a limb to earth. It wandered off up the track with a farewell look at its admirers.

We came across some elephants doing the soft shoe shuffle as they bathed themselves with dust and I have some nice footage of a large group swimming the Zambesi river.

We experienced a Hollywood style tropical downpour from the safety of our tents before breaking camp and heading for Zambia and Zimbabwe. Entering Zimbabwe, I was singled out to pay double for my visa, being one of the hated English race. We were the only buyers in the large market place and I felt so sorry for the vendors of what were well made stone and wooden figures of all sorts. When I bought a couple of souvenirs the grateful stall owner said his thanks for providing food for his family that week. How the country that used to be the bread bowl of Africa has degenerated into famine and despair. Mugabe must have a place in Hell awaiting him. Perhaps that is why he has clung to life so doggedly.

The Victoria Falls were quite spectacular, having not had sufficient rain to envelop us all in spray. There was some silly fellow swimming in a pool close to the edge of the falls. I would have loved to see him surging over the edge. What a shot! After pleasing filming we had a meal at the Victoria Falls Hotel. The poor staff were hard put to rustle up any food for us. I avoided what looked very like maggots and settled for the watery carrot soup. The main meal had three French beans and a very bony little fish and the fruit salad was a diced apple and nothing else. This was in a hugely smart hotel and really brought home to us to what level Zimbabwe had sunk. We were treated to some vigorous dancing by scantily clad natives as we left after five hours in the country. It had been an experience!

73

Literary Targets

BACK HOME IN Toowoomba I started a six month course aimed at improving my film script writing skills. Hal Croasmun from the USA has hundreds of students at any one time and must be very well off as his charges are not cheap. However the course is well structured and worthwhile, covering everything from the original script to marketing it, where I still have had no success, in spite of "Sam Fights Back" having won in two international competitions.

A typical agent gets about ten thousand scripts a year on his desk and if he gets to read yours, you are very lucky. They admit to reading only the first page in many cases and the first ten at the most. Readers are told to read twenty a day and to scrap ninety five per cent. So ones chance of success are infinitesimal.

Being the sublime optimist, I cater for the stray film producer or rich man/woman wanting to get richer reading this and so offer yet another short synopsis, this time of my Horror script, so shut your eyes.

In "Devil's Breed" a young city couple, Anton and Jenny inherit a Bush farm only to discover that all the land around them is owned by the charismatic cult leader, Davey. He has sold the farm they have just been left by Anton's uncle to a succession of buyers. Somehow he is back in possession of the farm again and again. Davey has a manic disciple who chases them through the woods at night when they try to escape their fate. Also a promiscuous female, who traps Anton when his drinks have been fixed at a woodland party. Anton is forced into slavery and a cage of his own. The Hoods, Davey's young acolytes, help subdue his victims and prove loyal to their master, even when one of their peers is to be sacrificed.

Not a film for the squeamish but Blair Witch, Wolf Creek and Stephen King have proved many times that there is a large section of the public that like to be frightened. This film I could produce for under $1.2 million, so join the queue to share in the profits. And don't blame me for the loss – of your innocence. You have been warned.

A friendly farmer, Lynnsay Fryer has offered me his farm on which to film. Three thousand acres in the Bush, it has a spooky atmosphere in places and would be ideal for virtually all locations. The target now is to find investors, who can afford a gamble. All films are high risk investments but Horror films have an excellent track record for making profits. Wolf Creek quite recently in Australia repaid its investors very well. Blair Witch cost $64,000 to make but took about $124 million at the box office.

Lynnsay started a cultural and moveable club. RUFFA. We navigated our way from playing music as a quintet to the birds in the Bush, to groups of artistic folk putting on little playlets in an antique hall about to be demolished; even doing our own things in the Rendez-vous café. If you could sing, you sang. If you had a poem to your name, you rendered that and hoped not to make too many squirm. Lynnsay is a big fellow so he had to buy a double bass to match. He plays a fair guitar – easier to carry – and roars around Queensland in an antique Land Rover, which is the only vehicle in which he can reach his farm in all weathers. Life as a farmer is tough and not lightened by ridiculous by-laws, which stop you from using your own water in your own dams, miles from anywhere without Council permission. He is also a talented artist, so I have invested in one of his paintings. He too has been a soldier, in the Australian army; a useful shot.

Lynnsay started a lunch-time musical group in the Settlers pub in Toowoomba. It was appreciated by the public and since we did not charge, the pub had an attraction, even if it did not advertise us. Sadly that faded.

Film Director's Course

A recent Directors' course arranged by Australian Film Base was held in Brisbane. I was one of the fifteen people attending and found it really worthwhile. We started by brainstorming a five minute feature film script and then three went away to write their own versions. Next morning one was chosen and after a quick introduction to Lighting, Sound and Camera work, we started by casting actors and choosing locations. The sound of traffic was an inhibiting factor. We had professional actors and make-up artists. Once we began the shoot, we took it in turn to do all jobs from Director to Grip, the person who sets up the camera gear. It was well worth the cost at about fifteen hundred dollars for five days. Even if one only produces short films in future, the same principles must be followed. The Director is King and no one makes suggestions apart from the D.O.P. (Director of Photography) while on Set.

To record all best shots and to check them on the monitor is essential. There should be an assistant director watching the monitor all the time, with a view to choosing the best sequences. An ulterior motive for attending the course was to find an experienced director, such as Chris Hobart, our tutor. The Film World is all about networking and creating the right crew is essential. I saw the necessity of having a professional camera and experienced Sound person. The continuity person and clapper board operator are equally important. Look out Bollywood. Here I come!

With ten full feature scripts available, surely one or two have a future. Ranging from Children's Action to War and Adult Action to Horror, there is plenty of choice.

Ralph Maddern of Focus Films, UK spent over a year working with me, free of charge on my seven episodes series for TV "Young Escapers," as he thought it a winner, but so far no luck.

74

Narrow Misses

LIVES SEVEN AND eight were used up recently, the first when I was returning from Jondaryan along that stretch of road with hugely wide verges. There are about twenty five metres of space on either side of the road. A heavy truck was close behind me when I observed a stationary car parked at right angles to the road. When I was about thirty metres away, travelling at about one hundred km per hour, the speed limit, the car suddenly shot across in front of me. Just as I was about to hit him, there being no time to swerve, it reversed out of the way, so I missed it by about two metres. I could not slow up with the truck on my tail but the driver did. The truck caught up with me about ten minutes later and I would have loved to have heard what he said to the car driver. He must have been on drugs or alcohol as he should have seen us approaching a kilometre away on the dead straight road.

The next brush with Death was even closer. I was travelling towards Brisbane one fine day again at about one hundred km per hour. It is straight and there are two lanes in each direction. Suddenly a car shot across in front of me, at right angles, so I had to swerve to my left to avoid cutting off its tail. I went onto two wheels as I missed its boot by less than a metre and then banged onto my other two wheels before thumping onto all four again. What on earth possessed the driver, who had a clear vision of my approach? I was really lucky to have reacted so fast. A very close shave!

Recently younger son Chris spent a few days with me and we motored up to the Carnarvon Gorge, an Australian icon. We broke the seven hundred km journey at Roma, staying at a splendid motel, The Explorer. It was both quiet and comfortable. Quite the best I have met. Arriving at the Gorge at around three o'clock, we just visited a local cave with a few Aborigine paintings and admired a semi tame wallaby. We slept in a batch with en suite. There was a frog in the loo of our first batch but then we found it was not ours; neither batch nor frog. The simple action of putting a number on the batch doors was beyond them. The food was good and it was a comfortable stay.

Next day we walked fourteen km and saw the Moss garden, not impressive, and a huge cave approached by steep iron ladders. We entered a sort of amphitheatre, bounded by high cliffs and marvelled at the birds flying and singing high. We had to cross the creek, about twenty metres a time, eighteen different times and with my balance problem, I fell off the small stepping stones twice but was only wet above the knees. It gave Chris something to laugh about.

We eventually reached a long cliff face with more intricate paintings although the skill was about Primary School level. The walk back seemed endless.

The return trip was a bit of an ordeal as we found Roma had no beds due to some football tournament, so having tried many pubs and motels I decided to motor the whole way back home, having only started at three thirty p.m. We stopped for a good meal at a café and reached home at eleven forty. Seven hundred km plus.

As I write this at an age when many are preparing for Bowls, Bridge and the Crematorium, I got together a musical group to play in the Empire Theatre, where I enjoyed Foster and Allen once again recently. Sadly our vocalist Ross pulled out due to ill health at the last moment. It was not meant to be. We are only on this earth once, so might as well make the most of it. It really was a treat having the Sound balance just right with this evergreen Irish duo. When The Searchers spokesman announced at the beginning of their show, with great glee that they were going to be loud, my heart sank. And they were! So one could not hear their great guitar player, nor the first rate singer... At least I think he was!

I should mention my Teens & School Leavers' Handbook I wrote to guide people of all ages upwards to avoid pitfalls and make the most of their lives. It is based on my own experiences and covers forty subjects, including making money out of property, surely of interest to most of us, sharing a flat, budgeting and many more essential areas. Had I been armed with such knowledge when in my twenties, I should have been a multimillionaire instead of just comfortably off. It sells at the princely sum of ten dollars a copy and every school should be using it as a discussion document to better the lives of their pupils. It might help put the drug barons out of business and don't assassinate me because the message is already out there. Otago University in New Zealand has it; also two of their leading secondary schools in Hawkes Bay. The Toowoomba Catholic Education Centre has copies. I am printing the third edition shortly.

One day I visited the Toowoomba show-grounds to see if anything was happening and found an American group of motorcyclists driving up ramps to fly through the air at breakneck speed. It was going to cost me $65 to get in and I only wanted to film for ten minutes so I asked two youngsters if I could pay them $5 to join them on top of their truck, which was parked in a strategic place providing an unobstructed view of the bikes. Thus I was able to get some excellent footage of bikes upside down narrowly missing others flying in the opposite direction. Moral of the story: Make your own opportunities!

Since I started this epic, south east Queensland has suffered its terrible floods, followed by much of the east of Australia. I was downtown, talking to Tony Wigan in the Rendez-vous cafe when the sky turned black. "I'm getting home, Tony" and I left. Already the streets were running six inches of water plus and all the way up to Middle Ridge. My garden was awash but luckily, being at one of the highest parts of town, my house was dry. Minutes after I had left, a block away there was the terrible tragedy of two boys and their mum stranded on top of their car, watched by helpless onlookers. A brave man rescued the youngest, when his elder brother said: "Take him first" and then both he and his mum were drowned. Still shops remained gutted many months later. Some seventeen poor souls were washed away in the Lockyer Valley below. One house was found 32 kilometres away.

At the time of writing we live in a world blown apart by September 11th. Travel will never be the same again, spoilt by luggage searches and body scans. I invariably set off the alarm at airports and immediately this dangerous old man attracts a body search. I must persuade my dentist to use less amalgam! I feel inclined to include another mercifully short poem, so suffer!

On returning to the UK after a surgeon in fitting me with a new hip in Toowoomba, left one leg ¾ of an inch longer than the other, and two mini strokes the same week, leading to a long neck operation, I have slotted into life near Worthing. The sunniest area in the UK, with a delightful bungalow, a ten minute walk to the sea, and a surfeit of activities on offer, life is good.

Needing a holiday before making the film, I went on a cruise with P & O round the Mediterranean. We visited Cadiz with its Flamenco dancers, Malta, Dubrovnik, Corfu, Valetta and Sicily to admire Mount Etna, quietly smoking with no government health warning. We ended with Gibraltar and its 36 miles of tunnels. All civilians were sent away during the war, but Italian bombs did little damage. A very relaxing and pleasant experience. Good entertainment every night and I received warm applause from about seven hundred people, when playing harmonica in the talent show.

The very strong South Downs Film Makers Club has enabled me to produce a 24 minute TV pilot film, "Young Escapers" the first of seven episodes where two 11 year-old boys run away from their foster parents and hide burglars' loot, starting a chase that will end in furthest Wales. It flows very well.

I hope to attract a producer into making the whole series. Very many thanks to our two stalwart cameramen, Bob and Richard, who shrugged off rain, to Howard, Editor and our Mr Fixer, who found an ideal location and two delightful boys, Paddy and Luke, and his co-Director, Brian, always alert to the best camera angle and really on the ball. Our first burglar, Nelson Ward, a professional actor, provided real expertise in acting, not burglary, while foster Mum Eileen scared the pants off the burglars while protecting her "litter". Howard doubled as foster Dad, extremely well and Tim, picked up to act in our local news-agents in South Ferring, was the kinder burglar, on his way to Hollywood! Jane did the lights and I was the rough Irishman, who gave the boys a lift to the next episode.

A World without War

Give up your bombs and guns.
Join the human race.
Try a little love.
Give Kindness a place.

It's cool to care for others.
Mankind are sisters, brothers.
It's cool to care for others.
Mankind are sisters, brothers

They send you out to kill
But stay at home quite safe.
They promise sex in Heaven
Join the human race.

Can God's messenger
Really be so cruel?
Get real! Wake up you fools!
Don't be the Devil's tools.

Give back their stolen land.
Provide them with a life.
End all prison walls.
Put an end to strife.

It makes one wonder whether there will ever be an end to this wasteful strife? What happens if the extremists take over the entire world, as they state their aim? God help the women. But whose god!

On a happier note, there are great steps forward by scientists towards eradicating disease and if enough of us pull together we may at least reduce Poverty because that is the breeding ground of extremism.

Why is it that as the world slides into a chronic shortage of resources, food and water, no one in high places says a word about the need to control population growth? It seems that China is the only country with a sense of responsibility. With over one billion Africans breeding at a huge rate and India not far behind, is it any wonder that we see pictures of starving children in masses, all expecting to come to the better off countries as if it is their right?

We hear daily from the righteous politically correct how we must absorb all these unfortunate refugees, but shouldn't their own countries bear some responsibility? Contraception, stop the corruption, spread their wealth more evenly, make Sri Lanka provide for the Tamils? Make the Afghan government deliver jobs for their own people with a massive drainage and water system improvement plan plus roads that you cannot dig up to place bombs? Cause is where attention needs to be paid; not results. Have none of the world's politicians got any brains?

Ignore these points for much longer and there is going to be not a boat a week approaching Aussie shores, but hordes of ships, daily. And there'll be nothing anyone can do to prevent them.

The Family

I HAVE DELIBERATELY kept quiet about my children's activities, not wishing to embarrass them with publicity. However an update: Tim has managed to collect a long list of qualifications including a Teacher's Certificate, a Degree, his R.A.F. scholarship, when he got his wings at eighteen, and celebrated by doing stunts over Canterbury Cathedral, which certainly were not on his game plan. He is a qualified driving instructor, he has passed all his Mariner's certificates and so can legally sail any small boat; not I think the Queen Elizabeth. He has improved various houses increasing their value considerably. He has a recording studio, composes music and plays tenor sax and various guitars. He has collected a wide circle of friends and lives in Brighton.

Caroline qualified as a state registered nurse; she has now a job in Surrey. She visits our relations in France quite frequently and appears happy with her lot.

Christopher has qualified as a diver and has worked in Tanzania for the government. He is currently working with the Home Office
in something confidential.

While writing this I have picked up an old book of my father's, Robert Graves, "Lawrence And The Arabs." He was a rebel and anti- establishment, and having read his "Seven Pillars of Wisdom, while serving in Ma'an in Jordan, I have always admired the man and felt a close affinity, although not wishing to emulate his self-starvation and incredible desert journeys. We are conditioned, as Nina and Frederick sung, to be in our little boxes, where most of us pass through life like clones, with the same targets, car, wife, house, children, etc..

I have never had any time for convention for convention's sake, saying the right thing, talking about safe subjects like Traffic and Weather, Sport and the latest camera. Is it any wonder people like the man I met in the street the other day are bored out of their tiny minds. When they reach retirement, some may look back on life and ask themselves what it all has been about.

Get out, young man and young woman and do your own thing. To Hell with those who disapprove as long as tomorrow you can live with what you did last night. It's your life and you only live once! Bond?

Hang Glider

Come glide with me through opal sky,
Free as the gulls, their plaintive cry.
So far below lie war and care.
Leave them behind for fools to share.

Throw down your guns, pick up a spade.
Let thoughts of war dissolve and fade.
Above the violence, bombs and pain,
Let's build a world of hope again.

Come glide with me among the clouds,
Free from crushing football crowds.
The swishing breeze – the only noise,
While far below explode their toys.

Come glide above the traffic jams,
The splashing boys, the babes in prams;
The courting couples haunt the lanes,
While Man imprisons Man in chains.

In writing this account of a life not wholly wasted, I must apologise to the many good friends and relations I have not included. They are not forgotten but I must respect their privacy and who knows, someone outside the treasured circle may read this.

If I survive, I may still have quite an addenda, since my parents lived to eighty nine and ninety, and my grandmother to ninety six. That's a threat!

My sincere gratitude to Phil Bell-Chambers, another easy to read author from Adelaide originally, who has come up with a page full of useful suggestions.

Also to Drew Grozier the Scottish author, who was enthusiastic having read this and always boosts ones morale. His "Scotch On The Bitumen" and "Blood Heritage" will appeal to Scots and Aussies especially. Also "The Umbrella Company."

My *"Tom In Trouble"* is now available on the Internet, and Smashwords. com has my *"Slave Children", "Vampire's Apprentice", "Tom In Trouble"* and *"Young Escapers"* on sale for downloading at $3/$4 a copy.

If you have reached this point, congratulations and may your god take good care of you.

Michael Faunce-Brown

It has been lovely hearing recently from past pupils. Keep them flowing. mrfbrown@hotmail.com

ABOUT THE AUTHOR

Michael Faunce-Brown, ex- soldier, farmer, teacher and currently a traveller, photographer, film producer, musician playing five instruments – not all at once – and writer of film scripts in the genres: Action, Thriller, War and Horror and novelist for adults and children, plus a part-time poet.

Also by Michael Faunce-Brown:

Against All Odds (Last Dawn), Fast Action, e-books via Smashwords.com plus Amazon et al.
Also in Pre-production as a film on Australia's Gold Coast.

Slug Bait, Thriller/Horror, e-books via Smashwords.com plus Amazon et al.
Also as a feature film script.

Slave Children, Fast Action, e-books via Smashwords.com
Also as a feature film script.

The Vampire's Apprentice (for 12+), Mild Horror. e-books via Smashwords.com

Tom in Trouble (for 12+), Adventure, e-books via Smashwords.com

Young Escapers (for 12+), as a TV script, 7 episodes, from mrfbrown@hotmail.com

Teens & School Leavers' Handbook, from mrfbrown@hotmail.com

Poems of Fun and Sorrow, from mrfbrown@hotmail.com

Lightning Source UK Ltd.
Milton Keynes UK
UKHW02f2208050118
315623UK00006B/322/P